THE
CAREFREE GARDEN

Letting Nature Play Her Part

BILL TERRY

TouchWood
Editions

TouchWood Editions
touchwoodeditions.com

LIBRARY AND ARCHIVES CANADA CATALOGUING IN PUBLICATION
Terry, Bill, 1935-, author
The carefree garden : letting nature play her part / Bill Terry.

Issued in print and electronic formats.
ISBN 978-1-77151-126-1

1. Native plant gardening. 2. Natural landscaping.
3. Low-maintenance gardening. I. Title.

SB439.T47 2015   635.9'676   C2014-908211-8

Photography: Bill Terry
Editor: Marlyn Horsdal
Proofreader: Claire Philipson
Designer: Pete Kohut
Cover image: *Trillium grandiflorum*, Missouri Botanical Garden
World map on page 45: free vector/Vecteezy.com
Author photo: Rosemary Bates

We gratefully acknowledge the financial support for our publishing activities
from the Government of Canada through the Canada Book Fund and the Canada
Council for the Arts, and from the Province of British Columbia through the
British Columbia Arts Council and the Book Publishing Tax Credit.

This book was produced using FSC®-certified, acid-free papers,
processed chlorine free, and printed with vegetable-based inks.

1 2 3 4 5   19 18 17 16 15

PRINTED IN CANADA

In memory of Carlo,
the under-gardener

Though an old man, I am but
a young gardener.
    —Thomas Jefferson

CONTENTS

1

Meet Mother Nature

T HIS STORY IS ABOUT MY idea of the perfect garden and
my efforts to create it. Or, I should say, *my* perfect garden. It
may not be yours. For while the meaning of perfect pitch can
be precisely tuned, and the perfect square is a fixed mathemati-
cal structure, the perfect garden—like the perfect face or human
figure—cannot be exactly defined. This book reflects my late-in-life
realization that gardening is not so much about creating *order*—as
most gardeners seek to do—as embracing a measure of *disorder*:
allowing plenty of room for serendipity, and seeking simplicity.

Welcoming serendipity may give rise to a happy accident (like
looking for a needle in a haystack and finding the farmer's wife). It
may be the consequence of an ant dropping a cyclamen seed in a rock
crevice, or a bird gorging on red huckleberries and then excreting
the seed on a rotting stump in the shade. It may be the fortuitous
outcome of the interweaving of different plants, producing painterly
collages of leaf form and texture, size and colour. Of course, moss,
lichen, and fungi are *all* serendipity, and all the more welcome for it.

In my perfect garden, simplicity means choosing plants of wild
origin over the fancy cultivars of the hybridizers—today's "hot plants."
It means, for example, growing species tulips from seed. By species
I mean those that evolved naturally, in the wild. Remarkably easy,

trouble free, and well suited to the aging or lazy gardener. I qualify on both counts. Simplicity is also expressed in excluding the super-showy performers, like that brilliant red rhododendron bush, screaming for attention. It blends better when not in bloom.

My idea of the perfect garden is a carefree garden. It's not a work of Nature, but it is much influenced by Nature, giving leading roles to plants native to the Pacific Northwest coast, where my wife, Rosemary, and I live. Accordingly, creating the perfect garden demands selective rewilding, the reintroduction of native flora that would very likely have grown here before the land was cleared or cultivated. They belong. Mother Nature insists on that. She is, as you will discover, a force to be ignored at your peril. So, right from the start, I advise engaging her as a full participant in the process.

But just who or what is this Mother Nature?

Call her Mother Nature, Earth Mother, Mother Earth, or what you will, the personification of Nature as a female deity embracing all creation in her loving arms has figured in human culture, worship, and mythology for as long as human society has existed. For the Greeks, Demeter was goddess of the Earth. In ancient Rome, Ceres was goddess of the harvest, fertility, and motherly relationships. The Huron called upon Aataentsic, the mother of humanity who fell from the sky and created the world. Among the Ojibwe, Nokomis, daughter of the moon, nurtured plants, animals, and humanity at her breast.

However, in casting Mother Nature in the role of partner in the performance of making the perfect garden, I needed to imagine a character I could relate to, not as a remote, ethereal spirit or an immortal deity, but one I could engage with directly, without the intervention of oracle, witch doctor, or priest. My imagined Mother Nature is entirely down to earth and not the mothering type at all. She's sharp-tongued, impatient, a bit of a fishwife truth to tell, a fussbudget with a voice as abrasive as a badly tuned bagpipe. As I got to know her, I found she had no time for small talk and absolutely no sense of humour. Don't kid around with this mother.

She appears in various forms, feathered or furred, but is always immaculately turned out, never a quill or hair out of place—consistent with her punctilious insistence that her instructions always be followed precisely.

The most annoying thing about Mother Nature is that she is always right.

The most curious thing is that, despite her irritating, uncompromising disposition, the more I got to know her, the more I came to respect her, even to like her. After all, in the end she did prove to be a sound advisor and reliable partner in the enterprise of trying to create the perfect garden.

2

The Perfect Garden

MY AMBITION WAS TO RETIRE as early as possible. Not because I hated my job: no, not at all. I loved it. Even so, I was not free to choose the what, the when, and the where of the working day.

I wanted to continue to work productively and purposefully, yet to own the freedom to do—as they say—my own thing: to choose the what, the when, and the where.

I wanted to reclaim my life.

We get only one appearance on this world's stage, and have no say over when the curtain falls. We can, though, ensure that the final act, the reclaimed part of life, will last as long as possible by slipping the bonds of paid employment as soon as we can afford to.

When I retired, aged fifty-seven, friends and colleagues asked why I was quitting so early; what was I going to do? "I'm going to create the perfect garden," I said. This proved to be an infallible conversation-stopper. As curiosity drained from their eyes, they would murmur "Really" or "How nice," make an awkward attempt to change the subject, or offer some excuse to shuffle off and find someone less loony to talk with. For how could anyone at the top of their form, immersed in the excitement of big city life and the cut and thrust of corporate engagement at a rather senior level, chuck it

The perfect garden.

all to take on such an effete occupation as *gardening*? Shouldn't I be taking on some worthwhile challenge—like saving the world?

Had I been asked, "Well that sounds interesting; what *is* the perfect garden?" I'd have been stumped for an answer. For I had no idea what the perfect garden was or what it would look like, what meaning it would have, what emotions it would stir. I just had some woolly idea that I'd know it when I found it. And I did find it: fifteen years later on the roof of the world, in the course of a plant-hunting expedition in the remote alpine meadows of the Himalayas. Not just once but repeatedly, as I attuned my eyes to the essential features of the perfect garden. I described it in my notes, during that once-in-a-lifetime journey, travelling by jeep through the mountains of Sichuan and Tibet:

"Every plant is in its proper place and never elbows out its bed-mates. No landscape designer has had a hand in its exquisite harmony. Irrigated with minerals from melting snow and fed with nutrients from decaying plants and organisms, it has no need for watering or fertilizing. There's no call for weeding because there are no weeds. A weed, after all, is the invention of the farmer or the gardener: simply a plant in the wrong place. A complex ecosystem in perfect balance, this garden sloughs off pests and diseases. It is never drenched with pesticides or fungicides. No gardener tends it. No cultivation is required. Nature takes care of pruning and deadheading. Indeed the very intervention of the gardener, bringing strange seeds and diseases in the mud sticking to the blade of his spade and the sole of his boot, introducing his own sense of taste and order, would unbalance, and eventually ruin the very elements that make this the perfect garden.

"In the perfect garden there's not even a whisper of industrial noise. The soundscape is silence, filled, as time and place determine, with dripping water, burbling stream, waves on the shore, birdsong, scuttling life, shivering leaves, and all the themes and variations of moving air.

"The perfect garden can be as small as a handkerchief or as large as the view extends. The perfect garden can be found in the icescapes of Antarctica, on the tundra blooming in spring, in deserts and marshes, in fungi feasting on rotting logs, in the curtains of orchids and other epiphytes that hang from the limbs of a tropical forest tree. It is found in coral reefs. It is found abundantly in the mountains on the roof of the world, the Himalayas."

Of course, as I wrote those notes, I knew that I was spinning threads of fantasy. To suggest that the perfect garden may be found in Nature makes as much sense as feathered fish. Other than for a few wackos whose beliefs orbit in the outer fringes of eco-freakdom, Nature has no consciousness, no concept of beauty, harmony, balance, or order. All these are in the eye of the beholder. Nature simply *is*. In Mother Nature's world, there's no such thing as a garden, perfect or not. By definition, a garden is an artefact, a thing made: a thing made by man.

The compositions I sketched as the perfect garden are works of Nature, nothing more: not works of art. However, these can, and do, and always have, and always should, provide us with inspiration—in imitation of Nature—to work toward creating the state of ecological equilibrium that the perfect garden represents.

Now, I'm not suggesting simply copying Nature, even if that were possible. What's the point? You can fill your heart with Nature by taking a walk in the woods or a stroll along the seashore. Besides, "A mere copier of Nature can never produce anything great, can never raise and enlarge the conceptions, or warm the heart of the spectator," said the painter Sir Joshua Reynolds in 1770.[1] He was referring to landscape painting, but his observation applies equally to landscape gardening. However, we should not resist being directed by Nature to some extent. We can let her own a part of the garden, even control a majority share.

Given that, the themes of the perfect garden should reflect the contributions of *both* partners. For Mother Nature: integrating endemic plants, choosing simplicity (natural species and varieties rather than cultivars created by plant breeders), and freely encouraging serendipity. For the gardener: building memory and expressing her own taste, creativity, and personality.

However, seeking to form a partnership between Mother Nature and the gardener is a challenge akin to mediating collaboration between the spider and the fly. For, as Michael Pollan, author and activist, astutely and bluntly observed, "Nature abhors a garden."[2] From the start, Ms. Nature sets out to thwart and destroy the gardener's efforts. The two are implacably opposed.

It would be essential, I realized, to come to terms with Mother, to appreciate and respect—above all *respect*—her point of view that in creating a garden I would be interfering with *her* world, not the other way round. She was here first, and, however battered, will still be here when we are gone. In planning the perfect garden, I would need to meet with Mother Nature, to show deference, to seek her advice. A touch of flattery might help.

I needed to make her an ally, rather than a foe.

3
Consider the Lay of the Land

1989. IT WAS FEBRUARY. ROSEMARY and I were visiting family in Vancouver and decided we'd rent a car and take a weekend to explore the Sunshine Coast before flying home, back east. It was one of those rare spells when an Arctic outflow, as the weather people call it, sweeps away the sullen, woolly overcast of the West Coast winter, chases the sun out of the closet, and brings a bite to the still air, with a sunrise sharp as a pin. But for that, we would not have taken a morning walk along the trail that followed the beach. Nor would we have wandered beyond the row of shorefront cottages and seen the undeveloped rocky slope above the trail.

"Now that," I said, "would be the perfect place to create the perfect garden."

Indeed, this land had very good bones. Part was enclosed within a curving cliff, five metres high, which embraced the property, sheltering it from the rumble of traffic and the sight of the small town beyond. We were merely a block from the highway and commerce, yet the dominant sound was the slapping of waves on the pebbled beach. The terrain was naturally terraced in weathered granite and thinly treed with arbutus and Douglas fir. Native wild roses, ferns, and salal had a footing in rock crevices, while huge granite boulders were all hung about with kinnikinnick and wild honeysuckle. Exposed bedrock was

Dry shorefront woodland: perfect bones for the perfect garden.

thickly carpeted with moss, or etched with greenish-grey bullseye lichen in runic inscriptions. What scant soil was there had never been turned. A few large, rotting stumps gave evidence of logging half a century before, but other than that, the land appeared to be little disturbed by human hand.

And then we saw the "For Sale" sign. And rather impulsively we visited the listing agent.

"Actually, that piece is not for sale," he said. "It's the one next door. They're owned by sisters."

He gave us a map and sent us back for a second look. The fact that he didn't bother to come with us indicated he thought it would be a waste of his time. After all, the property had been languishing on the market for over a year. We were enquiring about the wrong bit of land: surely not serious buyers. But we did take a second look, briefly explored the property as a whole and confirmed that while the half for sale was not quite what we were looking for, the other half was perfect. So, we returned to the realtor (much to his surprise), and put

Not a plant, lichen comes in many different forms and colours.

an offer on both properties, conditional on both being available. Then flew home, expecting we'd hear no more.

Two weeks later, the phone rang. "With a small adjustment to the offer, you have a deal." And thus, greatly astonished and delighted—though slightly queasy about our rash and impetuous decision—we found ourselves owners of an acre and a quarter of Sunshine Coast shorefront land that included forest, rock, and open meadow—miniature samples of different coastal ecosystems—gently sloping down to the Strait of Georgia, that part of the Salish Sea that separates British Columbia's Sunshine Coast from Vancouver Island.

To pay for it, we remortgaged our Toronto home and continued to work for the next five years, while visiting our land each summer, if only to make sure it hadn't floated away.

On one of those visits we found our architect in the Yellow Pages. "I'm retired," he said over the phone. "These days I'm only taking on projects with exceptional landscape and great views."

"Then you'll want to take this on. Come and see."

He met us on the land and agreed the site was worthy of his imagination. "I'm not interested in making a statement," he declared. "I don't like to blast rock. I don't like to cut down trees. I like to use local materials such as cedar. I like to design a house to fit the landscape, rather than the other way around." All these seemed good reasons to hire him, but the last was particularly important. For, whereas it often suits the developer or builder to clear-cut, blast, and bulldoze a rocky hillside into flat terraces with rows of tennis court-sized lots, the prospect of creating the perfect garden, as I have sketched it, is greatly improved if the gardener starts with a natural, largely undisturbed site, already furnished with native plants: trees and shrubs that belong there.

To begin with, our architect arranged a topographical survey of the property and sent us a copy of the resulting contour map, from which I made a three-dimensional, papier-mâché miniature representation of our land, and on that built a balsa wood scale model of the house that he designed for us. It was to be an unpretentious home of cedar and glass, with the very best view seen from standing at the kitchen sink. It would be a home well suited for a cook (her) and a gardener (me).

We kept this model on a table in the basement. We played with cardboard cut-outs, representing furniture, and imagined life in our future home, an indoor-outdoor home, just as it has turned out to be: though the house is not large, there are seven ways of stepping out into the garden. With its foundations pinned to the bedrock, our home belongs to the landscape and the landscape belongs to it. From outside, the glass reflects the varying mood and colour of sea and sky. From inside, as we look out on stormy mornings, the gulls shriek and the firs creak and sway. We sleep to a lullaby of wind and sea.

On calm mornings, crazy-coloured harlequin ducks perch on rocks at the shoreline. They have a theatrical scientific name—*Histrionicus histrionicus*. We watch Pacific loons, common mergansers, Barrow's goldeneyes, and, in winter, rafts of several hundred surf scoters. We have seen occasional red-legged black oystercatchers and once,

In spring, sea ducks head north to breed.

We look across the Strait of Georgia to Vancouver Island.

Tamiasciurus douglasii, Douglas squirrel.

silhouetted in the distance, a small paddling of bufflehead ducks, heading north in line astern. We have watched a school of dolphins skimming the choppy waves, chasing herring no doubt. Humpback whales or orcas occasionally cruise by. Over all, bald eagles preside.

We welcome the bushy-tailed Douglas squirrel, squatting on the deck, chewing the seeds from fir cones and leaving a scattering of husks. Not a tidy sciurine. This Pacific coast native thrives in areas not yet colonized by the black squirrel, the invasive tree rat that was introduced to Stanley Park, in Vancouver, from eastern Canada a hundred years ago.

In all, we took on a landscape, with its inhabitants, much as Mother Nature made it. She bestowed sheets of bedrock, a granite outcrop atop a cliff scarred with lichen, a meadow of spongy moss and licorice fern, and much more in the way of native trees and shrubs: a perfect stage for a perfect, carefree garden. We would be here for two decades, maybe three: merely passersby in the passage of time. Yet we had an opportunity to create—what?

4

Let the Moss Grow Under Your Feet

I SHOULD NOT LURE YOU INTO believing we had found the ready-made perfect garden. For, along with the native vegetation that belonged there, much of the property had been annexed by plants that did *not* belong: weeds, introduced at one time or another from other parts of the world. Especially, wherever the sun shone, our land was infested with invasive Scotch broom (*Cytisus scoparius*), a member of the bean family—botanically speaking.

We know who is to blame: Captain Walter Colquhoun Grant, a debt-ridden minor aristocrat, born in Edinburgh in 1821, a soldier and the son of a soldier. His father was the Duke of Wellington's chief spy at the battle of Waterloo. Disheartened with military life, Walter Grant exchanged the red tunic for a Scottish settler's rough tweed and bought passage to Vancouver Island in 1849. Rather than rounding the Horn, he crossed Panama by land; on the final sea leg, he rested in Hawaii, where he was greatly astonished and quite overcome with nostalgia upon finding Scotch broom in the garden of an old acquaintance, the British consul. Eager to recreate as much as possible of the flavour of his homeland in the New World (it is said he even tried to teach the native people Gaelic), Grant collected seed that he eventually scattered on land he purchased from the Hudson's Bay Company (HBC) at Sooke, west of Victoria, on the shores of the Strait of Juan de Fuca.

Scotch broom: shun its seductive charm.

Grant did not stick around to see the full consequences of his introduction. He was a restless and, by accounts, a feckless man. He abandoned his responsibilities as a surveyor with the HBC and the settler's life after only a year, and rejoined the army. Just imagine, though, how pleased he would have been to watch this yellow fever, Scotch broom, colonize southern Vancouver Island and eventually, the Pacific Northwest coast from northern California to Haida Gwaii. Now it is a well-established invader and, in some places, the cause of our native flora softly and silently fading away.

It's Time I Confessed to an Act of Eco-mischief

From our house we face out to a group of four small islands, the Trail Islands, about a kilometre offshore: rather too far to swim, but an easy crossing in a kayak. In 2014, you could buy one of the four for $1.98 million. For that price, the discerning buyer would have owned thirty-three acres and all the features of paradise that the real estate agency can cram into a hundred-word description. The Trail Islands are privately owned and uninhabited, aside from a few summer cottages. There's no ferry service, no roads, and no electricity or other amenities, so the prospect of established year-round residency is unlikely, at least for the foreseeable future. The islands are best known as a refuge for tugs to heave-to and snuggle in the shelter of the lee side in the event of stormy seas. The windward side is exposed to the wind and irascible weather of the Strait of Georgia, some fifteen kilometres wide.

Though not untouched by human activity, these islands are mainly as Nature made them, remarkably free of weeds. We have enjoyed paddling around and between them, drifting past small seal colonies here and there along the shore. In early summer, the pups are often parked for safety on rocky islets while mother is on the hunt. There are seabirds: red-legged oystercatchers, silent cormorants, Pacific loons, grebes, and the tiny, secretive marbled murrelet, a threatened rarity south of Alaska. Its nesting places were discovered in recent years, high on the moss-covered, weighty branches of a patch of inaccessible, and therefore never logged, old-growth Douglas fir on the Sunshine Coast. The decline of this bird, with its dependence upon old-growth forest, has made it a headline species for environmental activists. It lays just one egg per year, clearly an advocate of zero population growth.

One sunny day in late April, we kayaked to the islands, hauled out on the beach at low tide, collected oysters—for later swallowing off the half-shell, with a dab of fresh, grated horseradish—then walked along the shore to see what we might see. We were hailed by a woman, at work sowing seed and setting out annual bedding plants in her weekend cottage garden. Her enthusiasm was fetching, though the project was likely doomed for lack of summer rain. Here on the water's edge, only drought-tolerant plants are likely to survive. Scotch broom is one of these and, with pride and delight, she showed us several seedlings she had planted the year before, in full sun close to the high tide line: perfect conditions for establishing a beachhead for rapid colonization of the shorefront of this island, which up to now had been broom-less. These were blooming for the first time, she told us. And for the last, I thought to myself. Tactfully, I pointed out the potential consequences of her choice.

"Oh yes," she sighed, "others have warned me about that. But the flowers are so beautiful, don't you agree?"

I could tell there was no point in not agreeing. Those plants were there to stay as far as she was concerned, to grow into large shrubs, to go forth and multiply. We dropped the subject and continued our beachcombing.

In fall, the cottage season over, I kayaked to the island, ripped out all the broom and cast the plants into the waves. I hoped, indeed expected, that the gardener would attribute the loss to winter storms. In any event, this act of botanical sabotage achieved its objective. There is no Scotch broom on that island.

Gorse: a good-for-nothing noxious weed.

BROOM'S COUSIN, GORSE (*Ulex europaeus*), was also rooted in rock crevices on our land. Gorse, fondly known to the Scots as "furze," is also one of Europe's less welcome gifts to the colonies. Many wish it would return whence it came. It has established a bosky beachhead in rough and rocky places along the Pacific shores of southern British Columbia, where it arrived about forty years ago, having migrated from Oregon, the site of its introduction as an exotic ornamental early in the last century. The full menace of this spiny threat to our ecosystem has yet to be fully grasped. Its conquest of New Zealand may provide a warning. There, until 1890, seeds were sold for garden cultivation. Now, gorse has colonized that country to the point that three percent of sheep pasture and forestry plantations has been taken over by barbarous thickets, providing a business opportunity for an enterprising Kiwi who founded a company called Gorse Busters. He never lacks clients. Fire will not destroy it, nor will chopping it to the ground. It will grow back from the roots and must be grubbed out.

Moreover, our land had been well used for decades by summer

A pre-contact artefact.

picnickers and overnight campers, whose leavings included old car seats, a rotted mattress, condoms, and many reminders of the days when beer was sold in stubby bottles. The work of clearing out all this unsavoury refuse was mostly drudgery, but there were moments of discovery and surprise.

First, my nephew George, a labourer we imported from England as an indentured slave to help finish the house, walked over a yellow jackets' nest. He was wearing short pants and was stung in the naughty nethers. Poor George rushed howling into the sea.

Second, when I was hacking out broom rooted in a deep rock crevice, my mattock struck a flattish, rounded basalt rock, quite different from resident granite. It was buried two spade lengths deep. I pried it loose and saw that a hole had been bored through the thinner end. Clearly, this had been ground out from both sides. It weighed about three kilograms and proved to be an anchor. With a rope of cedar bark knotted through the hole, this rock would have served to moor a small canoe or, more likely, to secure one end of a cedar bark net stretched across the mouth of a creek. Long ago, a fishing party of Coast Salish might have camped here or paused to rest, and somebody carelessly left it behind. Given the hours and hours of painstaking work that would have been required, pecking away with shards of harder rock, to grind out the hole, I imagine that the person responsible for carrying the anchor would have been in deep doo-doo when its loss was discovered. Much as I was later scolded by an archaeologist friend for my undue diligence in scrubbing the rock clean and thereby removing all the organic matter that might have been used to carbon-date the artefact.

Well, having rid our land of broom, gorse, and several bins of exotic trash, what next?

We were familiar with the counsel of the eighteenth-century poet and satirist Alexander Pope. He was also a landscape architect, whose ideas of striving for harmony between the garden and Nature had considerable influence on the English landscape in his day. Seeking the spirit of the place (the *genius loci*) was an important principle in his thinking: the principle that landscape design—or for that matter garden design—should be adapted to the context in which it is located.

"Consult the genius of the place in all . . ."[1] he said.

There may be limited scope for such a fresh approach in taking on an existing garden. But starting from scratch, even when the builder has laid a light hand on the land, leaving it pretty well as Nature made it, few people planning a garden give much of a thought to the genius of the place. A lawn is usually imposed, surrounded with variations on standard themes of grasses, Japanese maples, weeping this and that, red rhododendrons, rounded blobs of purple heather, fast-growing hedges of laurel, photinia, or cedar, and accents of colour with annual bedding plants. Et cetera. If the land is not already suited to the conventional model, it may be made to suit with terraces, fill, and topsoil. Beware of topsoil. Even though sifted, it frequently contains bits of horsetail root that, once established, become your companion plants for life.

Where was I? Oh yes. Few people give a thought to the genius of the place and even fewer to the idea that Mother Nature might have a role to play. They should, because she can be the gardener's implacable enemy. As I have mentioned, in Michael Pollan's words, "Nature abhors a garden."[2]

Yes indeed. Imagine a garden from Mother Nature's point of view.

"Well, look what we have here . . . A richly fed, freshly dug and watered space, offering a juicy laboratory and an easy life for the explosion of all things gardeners hate: the seeding and proliferation of pesky weeds; the incubation and spread of pests and diseases, gorging upon plants raised and fattened in the controlled and sterile conditions of nursery greenhouses. Yummy!"

So, Nature will attack this garden. She will rain down plague and pestilence, frost and drought. She will summon winds to blow in weed seeds running amok. She will infest a lawn with chinch bugs, sod webworms, and June bug grubs, then fly in a murder of crows to rip up the turf in order to feed on them. She will do her damnedest to reclaim it as her own, which of course it once was.

Knowing this, in thinking about what to do with our land, I hit on the idea that this was a matter that just might be resolved through negotiation. So I imagined a meeting with Mother Nature over a decaf, fair trade, shade-grown, bird-friendly, organic cafe latte at the local Starbucks. She arrived late, elegantly decked out in brown and blue feathered finery. Something in her impenetrable black eye warned me she would be no pushover. Even so, we hit it off right away and quickly got on first name terms.

"Mother," I asked, "what should I do in my garden to work in harmony with you?"

"Simple," she replied, smiling sweetly. "Go native."

"Oh come on," I protested. "That's so *boring*. All those dreary conifers, salal, sword ferns, and stuff. That's not a garden. I mean . . ."

The air froze.

I must have said something wrong.

Mother Nature fluffed her feathers, *outraged*. "What! Are you blind? Don't you ever walk in the forest around here?"

Mother Nature.

Rhododendron macrophyllum, Pacific rhododendron.

I got the feeling this negotiation wasn't going to go my way—even though I was paying for the coffee. "What I *meant* to say was . . ." I began, but there was no chance for a rerun because I was instantly teleported to a shady gully three hundred metres high in the nearby forested hills.

"Just look around," warbled Nature. "Is this what you call dreary?"

She'd got me there. I had to admit I'd no idea that rhododendrons grew wild in our backyard. "You should be grateful," she murmured. "It's my special gift to the Sunshine Coast. You won't see them any further north." But we didn't linger long. Mother Nature whisked us off to another scene.

"Well? Is this boring to you, young man? This meadow of blue camas in spring? Are you one of those people who put down my efforts in this part of the world, simply because I caused an ice age twenty thousand years ago and snuffed out almost every living thing? Or how about sea blush? What's so boring about this lovely show?

"And here's a scene I'll bet you've passed by many times. Yes, and

Camassia quamash, common camas.

Plectritis congesta, sea blush.

Mimulus sp., monkey-flower.

Calypso bulbosa, Venus's slipper.

Lysichiton americanus, swamp lantern.

you were probably sitting in your car, too busy tweeting and twittering on your clever phone to notice this stunning sight in spring: showers of yellow monkey-flower and brilliant green moss cascading down the cliffs here at Horseshoe Bay, right where you drive off the ferry."

I raised my hands in surrender. "Okay, okay, Mother. I take it all back. I'm blindly insensitive, unfeeling, ignorant. I'm super, super sorry."

But her crash course on the allure of native flora was by no means over. "Just look at this Calypso orchid, also known as Venus's slipper. Could anything be more romantic? Stoop down and inhale the fragrance. How can you *possibly* call that boring? And what about this?"

"Aha," I said. "That one I *do* know. That's a yellow skunk cabbage."

Well, once again I'd put my foot in it. "A skunk cabbage! No, no, no. That's a *meadow lantern*. Shame on you for slagging such a beautiful thing."

Mother continued flitting about the woods, hovering a moment to show off her white fawn lily, drawing my attention to the delicacy

Erythronium oregonum, white fawn lily.

Nature's rock garden.

of its setting against well-weathered granite and patches of lichen. And next we cut to the seashore, to hail the beauty in miniature of the annual small blue-eyed Mary, named for the mother of Jesus. And then a rock garden, with sedums and monkey-flower and blue-eyed Mary again, as well as bits of fern and sedges and other plants not in flower that Mother Nature didn't have time to name for me. "You do the work. Look them up," she ordered.

And just to rub it in, Mother showed me that if your eyes are well tuned, you don't need flowers to find peace and harmony and colour and texture in her domain. It's there in bark, and moss, and lichen, and fungi—all to be found in the forests of the Pacific Northwest. Just walk in the woods to find inspiration for the perfect garden.

"Okay, I get it," I said, full of remorse that I'd given even a fleeting thought to the notion that going native would be boring or dreary. "Thanks, Ma . . ." But Mother Nature had vanished, and all I heard was the wind in the trees, a whispered sigh, "Don't call me Maaaaaaaaaaaaaaaaaaa . . ."

Subtle textures in the woods.
LEFT: Moss-covered artist's bracket fungus.
CENTRE: Exfoliating bark of arbutus.
RIGHT: Old-growth fir pockmarked by sapsuckers.

5
A Walk on the Wild Side

WELL, IF WORKING IN COOPERATION with Mother Nature was the aim here, she left no choice. I had to learn to recognize and give thanks for her gifts, and prepare to weave native plants into the fabric of our garden-in-waiting. This demanded—once the broom, the gorse, the broken glass, the trash of overnight campers was disposed of—taking stock of what already grew there. So Rosemary and I took a counterclockwise walk on the wild side, following the perimeter of our little piece of paradise.

It was April. Translucent arbutus bark, peeling in coppery sheets, was backlit by the thin afternoon sun: *Arbutus menziesii* (Pacific madrona), which we proudly display as Canada's only broad-leaved evergreen tree, is named in honour of Archibald Menzies, its discoverer. Menzies was a physician, and a botanist too. In 1790, he was appointed naturalist aboard HMS *Discovery* on her four-and-a-half-year survey of the northwest Pacific under the command of George Vancouver. It's likely that arbutus seedlings were among the collection of native plants that Menzies gathered and carefully tended in an improvised greenhouse on the quarterdeck. All perished from neglect, when the captain confined the botanist to his cabin for some unrecorded act of insubordination. It fell to the redoubtable Scottish plant hunter, David Douglas, to introduce this arbutus to cultivation in 1828.

Cones of the Douglas fir.

Underfoot, a dry crackle of fractured twigs, last summer's fallen leaves, needles, and cones. We admired the symmetry of the Douglas fir seed cones, with the "mice" scurrying to bury their heads under the overlapping scales. There is not quite enough space, so their hindquarters and tails are left dangling, easy pickings for any passing predator. The scales of the Douglas fir cone are spirally arranged in Fibonacci series (the golden spiral), wherein each number is the sum of the previous two (0, 1, 1, 2, 3, 5, 8, 13, etc.)—proof that Mother Nature can do math.

The southeast corner of our share of shorefront was marked by a fine amabilis fir (*Abies amabilis*), fittingly named, for *amabilis* in Latin means lovable. Coastal peoples boiled the bark, together with stinging nettle, for a tonic and for bathing, and treated colds with a tea made from the needles. They also enjoyed chewing the pitch for its sweet, spicy flavour. Though tempted, we haven't yet tried those remedies—but can confirm that tender new shoots of stinging nettles, foraged fresh in spring, lightly steamed, and served with a pat

Fragrant saskatoon blossom.

of butter, make a delicious green vegetable. Cooking kills the sting.

From there it was an easy scramble to a small plateau at the top of the granite bluff, where planes of lichen and moss, still soft and green from winter rains, blanketed the bedrock. Here, from the high point of our garden-to-be (*pace*, Mother Nature) were views in all directions: south over the roof of the house to the sea and the islands of the Strait of Georgia; east and north to the town and the mountains beyond; west to a quarter-acre fragment of Pacific coastal forest, well stocked with mature Douglas firs and western redcedars, still part of our land and providing additional privacy and shelter from noise. In all, what a glorious gift of Nature!

We paused to appreciate her generosity, standing well back from the five-metre, sheer drop-off, along one side of the bluff. We then followed a thorny but less perilous descent through snarly Nootka roses, still hanging onto last year's hips, oceanspray, and saskatoon bushes, newly leafed out and just starting to bloom in clusters of fragrant white flowers.

Saskatoon, *Amelanchier alnifolia*, is a deciduous small tree or shrub. So important was its fruit, the saskatoon berry, to the people of the northern Great Plains, that the city of Saskatoon was named for this plant, not the other way around. It has many aliases—Pacific serviceberry, western serviceberry, alderleaf shadbush, dwarf shadbush, juneberry.

Saskatoon berries rank so high on the nutritional scale that commercial growers are seeking to position them as a "superfruit," along with such fads as pomegranates, berries of the açaí palm, wild blueberries, and cranberries, all so packed with fibre, minerals, vitamins, antioxidants (which keep our bodies rust-proofed), and all things bright and beautiful that they will help you stay younger, grow stronger, live longer. Or so claim the marketers; the term superfruit has not received scientific validation. As for the saskatoon, it is said that the berry tastes like blueberry with raspberry, and a bit of apple. That may be true on the Great Plains, but in our part of its range, the fruit is strictly for the birds. It lacks flavour and is somewhat dry and pithy. Yes, the birds do love it. Bushes are quickly stripped of berries by robins feeding their young in summer.

We stepped off the bluff onto a broad area of bedrock luxuriantly padded with a deep mattress of moss, spongy underfoot. Different species were interwoven in subtle variations on a theme of green and yellow. This turf was elastic, yielding to a footfall, and then quickly springing back, unbruised. I have learned to love moss. It makes a mighty fine lawn, never needing watering or mowing, weeding or feeding.

One part of our mossy lawn was charmingly decorated with fronds of the licorice fern (*Polypodium glycyrrhiza*), rooted in rock fissures beneath the moss. This gets its common name from the licorice-flavoured underground stem, or rhizome, which was chewed by the Coast Salish (including our neighbours, or perhaps that should be our landlords, the Shishalh) for its pleasant flavour. Now we know why: the rhizome contains *osladin*, which is six hundred times as sweet as table sugar.

Moss makes a helluva fine lawn!

Fronds of the licorice fern.

This pretty native fern also grows epiphytically on the calcium-rich bark of the bigleaf maple. It flips the usual cycle of growth, being green in winter, then dormant in summer when the fronds shrivel and die. On our April survey, they were fat and fresh, their reverse sides painted with double rows of orange-brown spores. The licorice fern requires no care. Nature will attend to its minimal demands.

Nearby, the moss gave way to a patch of *Goodyera oblongifolia*, commonly called the rattlesnake plantain for its distinctive leaf markings. It was growing in the dappled shade of a rough-coated, old-growth Douglas fir. Native children would make little balloons by rubbing the leaves between their hands until the top and bottom separated, then blowing between the two halves to inflate them. Imagine that. It's actually not a plantain but an orchid, although to confirm that fact, you must examine the thirty-centimetre-high spike of numerous tiny white flowers with a magnifying glass. Then you see the characteristic orchid flower, with the hanging lower lip, like a surly teenager.

We continued our plant hunting, taking an inventory of the indigenous plants that Mother Nature had bestowed.

Beyond the sunny bluff and its buttresses of granite slabs and moss-blanketed bedrock, the rock abruptly ended, plunging beneath the forest floor, now deep, moist, and peaty, anchoring a coastal rainforest in miniature. No sunshine fell there. Only salal and sword ferns grew, the light being blocked by a dense canopy of mature fir and cedar, trees of a size that would make an ardent logger reach for the chainsaw. "Cut it, Burn it, Pave it," say the bumper stickers.

These trees deprived our northern neighbour of sun through the shorter days of winter, and he asked if we would please have them topped, "for safety." We declined, explaining that topping is the worst possible pruning practice, bad for the health of the tree and ugly besides. In the case of cedars, Nature reacts angrily, thrusting several new trunks skyward from the point of amputation. These become massive candelabras and, in the long run, a greater hazard in windstorms. Our trees, left untopped, grow taller, and our little forest remains undisturbed, an occasional refuge for wildlife. One summer, a black bear and her two cubs sought sanctuary in its dense shade for two or three days. We let them be.

Afternoon sun lit the fringe of this mini forest, the western boundary of our property. There, the conifers gave way to a fringe of alders and cherry, with an understorey of thimbleberry and thorny salmonberry (both of the raspberry clan) and red huckleberry, all parading their new leaves, all promising tasty fruit later in the year. Emerging into the light, we brushed off the spent petals of bitter cherry, falling like snowflakes from the trees above.

Our survey ended with an inventory of Nature's portfolio of plants along the southern side, our forty-five metres of shoreline. Thickets of leather-leaved salal flourished in pockets of thin, acidic soil. David Douglas, the heroic Scottish botanist sent by the Royal Horticultural Society to explore the Pacific Northwest, collected this invasive shrub and introduced it to Britain in 1828 as a garden ornamental. Guess what: there it escaped and greedily requisitioned heath and woodland habitats with tall and dense evergreen stands, often smothering other vegetation. (Come to think of it, perhaps the Brits introduced broom and gorse to us in retaliation.)

Within the salal, its parasitical partner, the Vancouver ground-cone, was hidden. All that's to be seen above ground is a stubby, purple-brown tumescence, much resembling a swollen fir cone. It's uncommon, an oddball sort of plant.

Here again, the showy Nootka rose (*Rosa nutkana*, named for Nootka Sound on Vancouver Island where it was first described) was well established on our property. In good soil, this can become very intrusive, exploring the neighbourhood with long, woody shoots running just beneath the surface—a form of colonization that is one of Nature's favourite strategies in reclaiming a garden. But in poor soil, or a confined, sunny space, let 'er rip, I say. We found the native bald-hip rose as well: *Rosa gymnocarpa* (bare fruit), with tiny leaves, tiny pink flowers, and tiny hips—a shy, shade-loving rose, quite in contrast to its brazen cousin.

An orchid, the western rattlesnake plantain.

The spiny Nootka rose, native to the coast from Alaska to California.

Oceanspray flowers in lilac-like clusters.

And we had oceanspray (*Holodiscus discolor*), with its creamy waves of pyramidal flower clusters. This native shrub, also known as ironwood, deserves our attention and appreciation. In Europe, after all, it's considered a desirable garden plant. Coastal communities hardened the long woody shoots with fire, polished them with horsetail stems and thus made harpoons, spears, and arrow shafts.

And finally we looked up, way up, to admire the native orange trumpet honeysuckle (*Lonicera ciliosa*), scrambling ten metres high through a bitter cherry tree that was just starting to leaf out. With roots in the shade and top in the sun, in a month this rampant vine would flaunt a cascade of tubular blossoms. Calling all hummingbirds! And there were red huckleberry, thimbleberry, salmonberry, saskatoon, salal, and Oregon grape. All of these were left alone and are still given free run, more or less, in the perimeter of our garden.

Taken as a whole, this may sound like a rich heritage of native plants. Well, it's not. We live in a part of the world deprived of the extraordinary floral variation that is characteristic of much of the southern hemisphere. A gardener in South Africa or Australia, for instance, can find great pleasure and satisfaction in creating a garden entirely from native plants. And it could be perfect, filled with flowers and foliage all year round. In Canada, though, we are impoverished (botanically speaking), due largely to the successive glaciations of the Pleistocene era, of which the most recent ended around twelve thousand years ago—a blink of an eye in geological time.

For this, I do blame Mother Nature. After all, the ice ages were her idea.

The western trumpet honeysuckle.

6
The Floristic Kingdoms

ARTH'S VEGETATION IS DIVIDED ROUGHLY into six floristic kingdoms, each a part of the world where plants have evolved in similar ways, isolated by geographic and climatic barriers, with similar plant families found throughout. The kingdoms are further divided into floristic regions, with similar plant genera, and these are again divided into floristic provinces, with similar plant species. Unlike countries on a political map, the boundaries of the floristic kingdoms are blurry. For, other than the Australian kingdom, which is entirely isolated by water, they merge into one another. This is not exact science. Transitional areas, where species from two kingdoms overlap, are called "vegetation tension zones."

Surrounding the South Pole, the Antarctic Floristic Kingdom includes, other than the continent of Antarctica (where only two flowering plant species grow[1]), Patagonia, most of New Zealand, and all the islands of the Southern Ocean south of latitude 40°S, except Tasmania where plant species are more closely related to the Australian Floristic Kingdom. Though now isolated by the vast Southern Ocean, half a billion years ago these scattered bits of the Antarctic Kingdom were part of the southern supercontinent Gondwanaland, which accounts for the close relationship of plant families.

Now, imagine yourself hovering some ten thousand kilometres

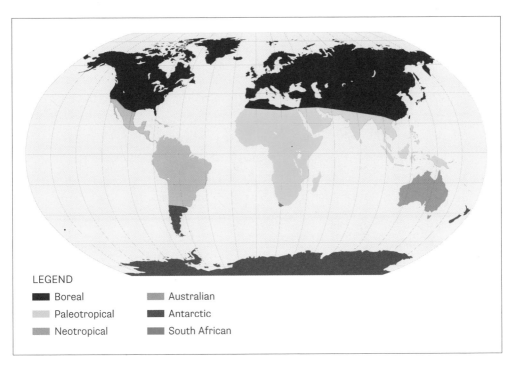

The floristic kingdoms.

above the North Pole. Spread beneath you is the top of the world: the Boreal (or Holarctic) Floristic Kingdom. It includes Europe, North America down to the Mexican border, and most of Asia: the northern hemisphere as far south as latitude 40°N, forty-two percent of the land mass of the entire world. All of this was at one time buried beneath hundreds of metres of ice, most of life extinguished. It takes time for evolution, in its infinite patience, to rebuild ecological diversity. Accordingly, in these parts, life is very young. There's a scarcity of *endemic* plants, meaning plants that evolved in the region, as distinct from those that moved north as the ice receded.

The Neotropical Kingdom, a realm of staggering ecological diversity, includes the southern tip of Florida, most of Mexico, the Caribbean region, and all of South America north of Patagonia.

The most prolific, as well as the smallest, of the six kingdoms is the South African Floristic Kingdom, a mere smear on the tip of the continent: ninety thousand square kilometres, a bit smaller than Cuba, just 0.04 percent of Earth's land area. This is home to more than nine thousand plant species of which about three quarters are endemic, found nowhere else on Earth. Most of this kingdom is treeless heathland, thickly covered with the unique, fine-leaved, evergreen vegetation known as *fynbos*. Among the indigenous plants that have evolved in the fynbos are about 660 *Erica* (heather) species and 1,400 different bulbs, of which 90 are gladiolas.

Across South Africa, there are ten national botanic gardens and they are *all* devoted exclusively to native plants, most of them displaying plants of the region in which they are situated. The most famous is Kirstenbosch, established in 1913 on the eastern slopes of Table Mountain in Cape Town, within the South African Floristic Kingdom. The original owner of the property was Cecil Rhodes, a principal performer in British imperial history. In 1895, he planted an avenue of camphor trees from China. This still stands, the only exotic planting in the gardens. It is said that Rhodes planted the trees in honour of Queen Victoria, to represent the outposts of the British Empire. He hoped Her Majesty would visit the Cape. She never did.

In Canada, part of the Boreal Kingdom, Mother Nature has relatively little to offer. There is *no* botanical garden devoted exclusively to the conservation and cultivation of native plants, although the Royal Botanical Garden in Burlington, Ontario, comes close. Otherwise, in this country's botanical gardens, native plants generally hang their heads, somewhat apologetically, in a remote and often neglected corner of the estate.

Compare this with the Paleotropic Floristic Kingdom, in particular South Africa.

In early 1999, Rosemary and I flew to Johannesburg to begin a seven-week-long, 7,500-kilometre trek, the length and breadth of South Africa, driving a small rented car. Nelson Mandela was close to the end of his term as president, four and a half years after the peaceful close of the apartheid era. The country was still in a state of euphoria, though some Afrikaners acknowledged they were keeping their powder dry. We drove east, in the direction of Kruger National Park, where we would stay for nine days. Our first stop was a private,

South Africa, looking east from the Klein Drakensberg.

two thousand-acre game reserve, high in the Klein Drakensberg mountains. We stayed in a *rondavel*, the traditional African round hut, with walls of clay and stone and a thatched roof. We were glad to share our accommodation with a family of geckoes that clung to the inside walls with sticky feet and helped keep moths, mosquitos, and other bugs reduced to a dull roar.

One day, I booked a botanical tour of the reserve with a Rhodesian-born botanist, the first of several people we met who had moved to friendlier (for whites) South Africa, when their country was renamed Zimbabwe, under black rule.

"Wear boots," he instructed. "There may be cobras, puff adders, and other poisonous snakes. Bring a hat, water bottle, notebook, and pencil. We'll be gone for five hours."

He picked me up at eight o'clock in the morning, a man older than I, but hardened by daily hikes in the reserve. I followed him uphill, through savannah and forest, scrambling up steep sandstone, a thousand metres to the top of an escarpment. There, a breathtaking view to the east—as if my breath was not already taken by the effort to keep up. We could see across the lowveld to Kruger Park and maybe even beyond into Mozambique.

"Look around. There's a greater number of endemic plants in this reserve than you'll find in the whole of the British Isles," my guide declared. He might equally have referred to the whole of British Columbia. For the more I saw, the more I realized what meagre fare Nature served up at home.

He introduced me to some of the wonders of evolution in a landscape never scarred by ice ages. He knew every inch of the hillside and we stopped frequently for a short lecture.

He explained the intricate mutual dependence of the wild fig and the fig wasp. He demonstrated how to get "soap" from the soap nettle. He showed me that bitter aloes is a yellow fluid secreted by the outer skin of the fleshy leaf of *Aloe ferox* ("taste it"), while the core produces the sap used in cosmetics and salves. He introduced me to a tree that is so poisonous that even burning the wood will make you sick if you inhale any smoke. I ended the walk with fists full of aromatic leaves, natural "Velcro" leaves, berries and small fruits to share with Rosemary. Even so, my guide was in despair over how little of the indigenous vegetation remains undisturbed, outside the reserve.

"All around, the native flora has been burnt for firewood, trashed by cattle, invaded by alien species such as lantana and prickly pear, or replaced by commercial plantations of foreign pine and eucalyptus. It seems whatever man touches, man destroys."

During our long South African safari, we were surprised to see how few gardeners made use of the prolific variety of native trees, flowers, and shrubs. Rather, most chose to grow roses, dahlias, bougainvillea, canna lilies, and petunias: exotics all. Distant pastures always look greener. Nature, presumably, abhorred these gardens, and doubtless the gardeners, like many in those days, fought back with an arsenal of weapons of mass destruction (WMDs): herbicides, pesticides, and fungicides. They could have gone native instead.

If I were living in almost any part of the world other than the Boreal

Floristic Kingdom, I could set out to create the perfect garden using exclusively plants native to the region.

But back home, going entirely native was not going to happen—no matter what Mother Nature demanded. Some gardeners would disagree, but, to my eye, there simply isn't enough native plant diversity where I live, in the Vancouverian Province of the Rocky Mountain Region of the Boreal Kingdom, to make an interesting, satisfying, year-round garden, perfect or not.

7
Rewilding

DESPITE THE LIMITED REPERTOIRE OF native plants suited to our particular site, I knew I had to make the best possible use of them.

Mother Nature had made that perfectly clear. "Go native," she had said. And she meant it. No doubt about that. From our first, somewhat humiliating, encounter, I had learned that she was crusty, demanding, not easily given to compromise, a bit of a bully. But really we were not at odds. As I said earlier, the perfect garden begins with the inspiration provided by her landscape and her choice of plants. That's the foundation. From that starting point we may modify; add pond or stream for example; shift rocks to build walls and steps, or place them for artistic effect. We may make pathways, even discreetly and selectively introduce plants from other places—while all the time taking pains to keep Mother on side.

Another feature of the perfect garden is that it is easy-care or, better still, care-free. This is entirely consistent with the requirements of native plants. They belong here. They should flourish with little or no attention, and should survive summer drought with little or no watering. They can be expected to be resistant to the ravages of pests and diseases. Naturally, most will self-propagate by seed or root without the intervention of the gardener.

Certainly, working in partnership with Mother Nature was the key to success in creating my carefree, care-free, perfect garden and going native was the starting point: seeking to augment what was already established by restoring what might once have been growing there. For a start, the spring-flowering bulbs: fawn lilies, chocolate lilies, trilliums, black lilies, crown brodiaea, blue camas. Reintroducing these would be a very modest example of what is now called *rewilding*.

Of course it was unthinkable to dig up these bulbs in the wild. Over the decades, this malpractice has already done quite enough damage—to the point that nature lovers will often keep secret the location of special plants, such as the mountainside glade of *Rhododendron macrophyllum* that Ms. Nature had shown me during our first encounter. Nor are they generally offered in garden centres, but for a handful of specialty nurseries. Besides, we need to grow these *en masse*, as in the wild, and that becomes very expensive. Where do the specialty nurseries get them? They grow them from seed. We can do the same. It's Nature's way. But we can do better than she does, simply by giving every seed a good chance for germination and survival, whereas in the wild only a tiny fraction will make it, the majority falling on stony ground, to be eaten or washed away.

People protest they haven't the patience. True: it will take three or four years to produce a flower from the seed of these native wildlings. So regard it as a long-term investment, like buying bonds. Buy a bond every year. Start some seeds in a pot every year. There are annual dividends: signs of growth. A grass-like shoot from each seed in the first spring; a true leaf in the second; a cluster of leaves in the third; a beautiful flower in the next when you proudly declare to your gardening friends, "I grew that fawn lily from seed." Or even, "I grew that peony, that rhododendron, that magnolia tree from seed." In that, there is immensely more satisfaction than showing off a nursery-bought plant.

Growing Native Spring-flowering Bulbs From Seed

Ingredients
- *Patience*
- *Seed*
- *One-gallon-sized square plastic pots (they take less space than the round ones)*
- *Sterile, well-draining compost (e.g., Sunshine #4)*
- *Coarse grit or sand*

Collect seed when ripe in summer. Sources include wild plants (be sparing), other gardens, seed exchanges. Start seed in late summer or early fall, in a pot filled with moistened compost to about four centimetres (an inch and a quarter) from the top. Tamp it down. Scatter the seed on the surface. Be liberal, because bulbs are more or less rootless when dormant, so that even if they're crowded it's easy to separate them when the time comes to transplant. Cover the seed with a thin layer of the same compost and then fill to the top with grit. The grit helps discourage the growth of moss, liverwort, and weeds, and acts as mulch, keeping the seed surface cool and preventing rapid evaporation.

Leave the pot outside in the shade, protected from slugs. Ideally, put it on a wire rack so that it will drain properly. Do not bring it indoors or into a greenhouse, even in the event of frost or snow. Nature does not do that. Neither do we. All being well, in spring there will be single grassy shoots, a pinhead bulb attached to each. Do not disturb. Simply sprinkle a pinch of slow-release fertilizer on the surface and leave the seedlings in the pot. Come the following spring, they will reappear, bearing one or two *true* leaves. Wait a few months until these leaves wither and die down in mid- to late summer, a signal that the bulbs are dormant. Then it's time to tip out the pot, carefully separate the little bulbs, and transplant them either to the garden (about five centimetres deep) or to small (ten-centimetre) pots. Three to a pot.

Just make sure to plant them the right way up.

I WAS ON my knees, working on a moist area of the spongy moss lawn when a red-shafted flicker, an ambassador of She-Who-Must-Be-Obeyed hopped onto the scene.

"Hey, what's up, man?"

"As you can presumably see, I'm peeling back a big sheet of moss here."

"Whatever for?"

"Well, the plan is to spread a bucketful of sterile compost on the bedrock, scatter pink fawn lily seed over that, and then replace the moss. The seed will germinate, and eventually each spring, the flowers should bloom in a bed of moss. Anyway, that's what I'm hoping. Rewilding you might say, on a very small scale."

"Cool. But don't you know that *Erythronium revolutum* never grew here? In Canada, the pink fawn lily is confined to Vancouver Island."

"Picky, picky," I said. "Please tell Her Royal Blueness that if she's going to restrict me to native plants found on the Sunshine Coast, we're not going to get much of a show. Let's agree on a larger region, say the Pacific Northwest coast."

I was expecting to fend off a charge that that would not be rewilding, insofar as that term, strictly speaking, refers to restoring habitats to their natural state. But my feathered friend wasn't listening. She was flying at a feeder designed for smaller birds, chickadees and nuthatches, and filled to the brim with sunflower seed. Her efforts set the feeder swinging, causing half its contents to spill. "Mighty toothsome," she whistled, deftly separating seed from shell. I took this to be assent and completed the experiment. In time, pink fawn lilies flowered exquisitely in the moss.

From seed, I grew their equally exquisite, though larger, cousins, the white fawn lilies (*Erythronium oregonum*), which had been shown off by Mother Nature during our first encounter. The leaves, she had pointed out, are spotted, much like the camouflage of a fawn. Their range includes the Sunshine Coast and they settled down pert as could be in a part-shaded rock crevice, a setting chosen in

Erythronium revolutum, pink fawn lily.

imitation of Nature. And indeed, who could detect that this troupe of tutu-skirted ballerinas was an intentional work of man (a garden) and not an unintentional work of Nature (wild)? Leave the fawn lily alone, let the surrounding rocks gather moss and it will re-seed itself and multiply, arguably *becoming* wild, requiring no care as Nature takes her course.

Again, originally started from wild-collected seed, the chocolate lily (*Fritillaria affinis*) now flourishes here and there in our garden. These days I just collect my own seed in summer and fling it about in dry and sunny places. I don't even bother to rake it in.

The western wake-robin (*Trillium ovatum*) was also quite easy to reintroduce in dappled woodland shade. Extra patience is called for, since it can take as long as three years for the seed to germinate. Once established, however, it's altogether trouble- and maintenance-free and can live for seventy-five years. So, I like the thought that the patch of western trilliums I have reintroduced should long outlive me, standing as a memorial of sorts. More likely

LEFT: The chocolate lily, a fritillary variable in colour.
RIGHT: The western trillium opens in white and fades to reddish-purple.

though, it will be buried under acres of concrete. Meantime, here in our garden, it seeds itself, and very slowly spreads.

The beautiful black lily is quite a rarity hereabouts; a native fritillary whose location in the wild on the Sunshine Coast is a salt marsh, known only to a few (and we aren't telling). Its range, however, is extensive, ringing the north Pacific coast from Oregon to Alaska to Siberia, Kamchatka, and Japan. It's sometimes called "rice lily" or "northern rice root" because the scaly bulb is wrapped in a cluster of tiny, rice-like bulblets. Grown from seed, it makes a home in our garden, flowering in a sunny rock crevice where water tends to collect. Coastal peoples used them in a variety of delectable recipes. The bulbs were boiled or steamed, baked or ground to a paste, added to fish or meat stews, served with oolichan oil, even eaten raw with fish eggs—presumably as an appetizer. Regardless of the recipe, the bulbs are extremely bitter and must first be soaked for hours in several rinses of water. It also has the misfortune to have a noisome stench, hence certain uncouth pioneers with no

One of two native fritillaries, the black lily.

Crown brodiaea blooms after the leaves have died.

appreciation for the finer things of Nature tagged it "dirty diaper" or "outhouse lily." These monikers are undeserved. *Fritillaria camschatcensis*, in flower, is a thing of beauty. Just hold your breath.

Scattered bulbs of crown brodiaea (*Brodiaea coronaria*) were lurking in the grass on our shorefront. Again from seed, these were very easily propagated and introduced to the garden, while the loveliest native bulb of them all, the blue camas lily (*Camassia quamash*) was also re-established—a meagre contribution to rewilding, considering the one-time abundance of this plant, now greatly depleted due to urban and agricultural development. Here's what Meriwether Lewis, the American explorer, beheld in Idaho, not far from Washington State, on June 12, 1806.

"The quawmash is now in blume and from the colour of its bloom at a short distance it resembles lakes of fine clear water, so complete in this deseption that on first sight I could have sworn it was water."[1]

At best, I might restore a puddle of fine clear water.

LEFT: Blue camas lily.
RIGHT: Meadow death camas.

FOR OUR REWILDING effort, all these native bulbs were started in pots from wild-collected seed and then, after two years, set out and left alone in areas of our property that provide conditions reasonably similar to those that suit them in the wild meadows and woodlands of the Sunshine Coast. It was so easy.

I even found a damp place to grow the sk . . . oops—meadow lantern (*Lysichiton americanus*). Again, easy from seed.

The skunk cabbage, as most people call it.

Cultivating Camas

For native people, along the coast and elsewhere, camas bulbs were an essential source of food, a staple so important that they were carefully conserved. Only the larger bulbs were harvested, the smaller ones being left to grow on, the seed collected and scattered. The people learned (after who knows how many fatalities) to make a clear distinction between the edible camas lily and the deadly poisonous death camas (*Zygadenus venenosus*), potentially lethal to man or meadow-browsing beasts. It's especially dangerous to domestic sheep—introduced animals that did not evolve with the killer bulb and are too stupid to learn from experience. Even honeybees are poisoned by its nectar or pollen.

The bulbs of these two lily family plants are similar in shape and size and easily confused. However, in spring when they flower, for anyone with eyes to see, the distinction is clear. For the death camas has a tight, terminal cluster of white flowers, similar to an onion in bloom and very different to the blue spike of *C. quamash*. So, to avoid any chance of disastrous error, camas bulbs were usually harvested while still in flower.

8

The Double-flowered Salmonberry

SO FAR, ALL SEEMED TO be going well. Presumably, Nature saw that it was good. All the native plants were flourishing and healthy. No bug onslaughts. No diseases. The only objections were voiced by a raucous chorus of dive-bombing crows, trying to scare me off if I worked too close to their nests.

All these native spring-flowering treasures thrived and survived the vagaries of our uncertain weather. So I invited Mother over for a further consultation, rather expecting she would let me get on with growing *real* garden stuff without interference. But I wasn't going to get off that lightly. For one thing, it seemed she didn't think these efforts were worthy of a personal inspection. Instead, she sent a deputy, a Douglas squirrel that I caught trying to dig up the bulbs I had so painstakingly raised.

"Enough of that," I said. "I didn't raise these bulbs to feed hungry scatter hoarders. What's the word from Mother Nature?"

My furry friend was blunt. "She says she can see you've made a token effort with the spring bulbs, but aside from that, you haven't shown her anything she hadn't already put there—the roses, the honeysuckle, and all that. She says you've been wasting time growing crosses of dahlias, ridiculous tulips, fancy daffodils, hybrid tea roses, chrysanthemums, all of which you know she abhors. She says if you're serious about working with her you'll get serious about reintroducing other native plants: shrubs, trees, perennials. She insists that you grow mock orange, the tall Oregon grape, snowberry, and evergreen huckleberry, all of which will do well here. She wants to see native trees and ground covers. She wants to see flowering currants to feed the rufous hummingbirds in early spring."

Yikes!

Well, as it happened, I'd been eyeing a partially shaded strip of public road allowance adjacent to the lane that leads to our place and on to the beach. It had been neglected for decades and, although safe sanctuary for nesting songbirds, was a towering tangle of botanical nasties: Himalayan blackberry, Japanese knotweed, bindweed, the holly and the ivy, periwinkle—all exotic escapees from cultivation and *all* listed as invasive species in our region. Our plan had been to convert this to a showplace of rhododendrons, but instead we recognized it would make a fine gallery for the Pacific Northwest coast creations of Mother Nature, with the added advantage of giving pleasure and inspiration to passersby. We had no difficulty in getting the approval of the municipality for transforming this thicket of weeds into an arboretum of native trees and shrubs, and we enjoyed the enthusiastic support of the newly founded Sunshine Coast Botanical Garden Society.

And so, one winter, I took mattock and spade, and bit by bit grubbed out all trace of the knotweed and the bindweed, the blackberries and the bracken, root and branch, and, over time, with immediate removal of any new shoot—any attempt by the nasties to recolonize the area—managed to get rid of them entirely and forever. Fittingly enough, all that remained standing was the only native plant, a Pacific dogwood tree (*Cornus nuttallii*), the official floral emblem of British Columbia, protected until 2002 when the law was repealed.

The following spring, with assistance and bountiful contributions of homegrown native plants from our botanical friends, we set out the

NORTHWEST COAST PLANT HABITAT
DEMONSTRATION GARDEN
A PROJECT OF
THE SUNSHINE COAST BOTANICAL GARDEN SOCIETY
AND THE DISTRICT OF SECHELT

Partnership with local government was necessary (this was public land), and also judicious, since it made it less likely that the authorities would turn this road allowance into parking stalls for beach users. The mayor himself demonstrated support at the opening ceremony, by climbing a ladder and attaching the sign to the dogwood tree.

The plants, without exception, flourished. And thrive still in the deep, damp, shady soil, enriched by at least a half century of leaf mould and topped with about fifteen centimetres of bark and wood chips. The leaves fall where they may and rot where they fall. The space is never watered or fertilized, let alone sprayed. There are no slugs.

The first to bloom, in early spring, is a fragrant flowering shrub, the pristine white form of the normally red-flowering currant, *Ribes sanguineum*. While the white version is occasionally found in the wild, this is more likely a cultivated selection, 'White Icicle'. Luckily, Ms. Nature was not too persnickety and allowed this variation. Soon after, the more familiar—and definitely native—red form is in full bloom, a signal for the return of the rufous hummingbird, plunging its long bill and flickering tongue into the throat of the flower to lap the sweet nectar,[1] just as Mother Nature wished.

The two resident species of Oregon grape make a home together in this native garden. They're known as the tall Oregon grape (*Mahonia aquifolium*) and the dull Oregon grape (*Mahonia nervosa*). Actually, they are not grapes, not even closely related. But the clusters of purple fruit in summer are somewhat grape-like, and

Ribes sanguineum, 'White Icicle'.

people do make wine from them. More commonly, they make an excellent jelly. I particularly like the holly-like evergreen leaves— shiny on the tall, matte on the dull—and, above all, the clusters of intensely scented yellow flowers that light up the bushes in spring.

A seed from the Pacific rhododendron (*R. macrophyllum*), taken from the mountainside glade that Mother Nature showed me when we first met, germinated and grew to become a sturdy, pink-flowering bush. Some of the leaves, close to the ground, are notched by weevils, but I let them be, in keeping with the principle of letting Nature play her part.

When it's in bloom, one spectacular shrub stops passersby in their tracks. It's a double-flowered salmonberry (*Rubus spectabilis florepleno* 'Olympic Double'), grown from a cutting. The flowers, in late spring, are like magenta roses, five centimetres across. Like its parent, the widespread common salmonberry, it produces a scanty crop of raspberry-like fruit, too bland to be worth more than casual picking, but unlike the parent, in bloom it's a joy to behold. I tried

Red-flowering currant, harbinger of hummingbirds.

Fragrant flowers of the tall Oregon grape.

Juicy fruit of the dull Oregon grape.

Pacific rhododendron, the state flower of Washington.

growing the double form from its seed, but the offspring all reverted to the parent type, which is an invasive brute. It's welcome in the wild where it quickly claims forest edges and stream banks, as well as moist, newly cleared areas—but it's on my no-fly list in a small, *cultivated* garden of native plants.

Along with the dogwood, trees form a canopy. There's cascara (*Rhamnus purshiana*), a small tree whose numbingly bitter bark is scientifically established as an effective laxative. We planted a seedling of the Sitka mountain-ash (*Sorbus sitchensis*), which grows along the entire BC coast. This quickly became a tree, bearing bitter berries, which, it is said, the Nuxalk of Bella Coola crushed, then rubbed the juice into the scalp to fight lice and dandruff. While still within the Pacific Northwest habitat, we stretched the definition of native plants, and reached into southern Oregon to include the tanbark oak (*Notholithocarpus densiflorus*), a fast-growing evergreen tree that is, in fact, not an oak; it's so nicknamed for its acorn-like fruit. Unfortunately we'll never see the fruit, because

The double-flowered salmonberry.

The superstitious believe that smelling the spots on the Columbia lily can give you freckles.

after about ten years, it had grown so dense, so tall and wide that it was shading out several precious shrubs of coastal British Columbia. I asked forgiveness of Ms. Nature and picked up the chainsaw. Within weeks, Herself protested by producing a shower of new shoots from the sawn-off stump. So stubborn! We settled for letting the tanbark oak make a comeback as an evergreen shrub.

The mid-storey shrubbery, besides flowering currant and Oregon grape, includes mock orange, evergreen huckleberry, saskatoon, oceanspray, snowberry, and snowbrush, a white-flowered species of California lilac (*Ceanothus velutinus*).

In late spring and early summer two showy, orange, perennial wildflowers keep company in this native garden: the Columbia lily and the western columbine, both easily grown from seed. The lily (*Lilium columbianum*) has edible, though somewhat bitter and peppery-tasting, bulbs. The columbine (*Aquilegia formosa*) attracts hummingbirds. The flower, wearing a crown of orange-red spurs, is edible and sweet tasting, but don't eat the shiny black seeds. Consequences can be fatal.

At ground level, in early March, we can expect to see the mottled rosettes of the white fawn lily emerge from the leaf litter and, within a month, its shy, pendant flowers unfurling. At the same time, the broad-leaved starflower (*Trientalis latifolia*) emerges from winter dormancy and pops up all over the place with tiny, six-petalled, white flowers, tinged with pink, held aloft on a threadlike stem. This delicate plant is also known as Indian potato, a name that would generally be considered politically incorrect these days. However, it does produce knuckle-sized tubers that were gathered for food by some coastal groups. Despite its proliferation, it is no threat to other plants. Nor is false lily-of-the-valley (*Maianthemum dilatatum*), which has no inclination to seek the sun, preferring to hide in the deep shade of the cascara tree. In May, blue camas lilies duke it out with Pacific coast native irises. The latter cross promiscuously in the wild as well as in gardens, creating hybrids that flower in blue, purple, gold, and white.

I planted two native ground covers—Pacific bleeding heart (*Dicentra formosa*) and redwood sorrel (*Oxalis oregana*).

"Big mistake," whispered Mother. "Get rid of them. In soil this good I'll set those two running amok all over the place. Soon they'll choke all those little treasures you're so proud of, like the fawn lilies, the chocolate lilies, and the trilliums. Just watch me."

Good advice. Native plants, too, can become invasive, gobbling up space, if planted in situations that offer abundant nutrition and no competition for their foraging underground runners. I dug them up. Simply planting out native plants by no means ensures *balance*, one of the essential features of the perfect garden. In the most unlikely event that this garden is neither paved over nor eventually reclaimed by the exotic nasties, it would take years to establish ecological equilibrium, to determine which of the trees, the shrubs, the perennials, and the ground dwellers (now all fighting for space and light) would survive. Moreover, this is *not* exactly rewilding: in Nature, the cascara has no business sharing turf with the arbutus; the California lilac would not likely congregate with the Pacific dogwood.

It's not a *no*-maintenance garden. There's no such thing. But it is a very *low*-maintenance garden. Weeds scarcely get a look in, but for occasional seedlings of laurel, oak, or blackberry, from seeds dropped in bird poop or stashed by squirrels. I pluck these, but otherwise generally let things be. So the columbines self-seed and form clumps, and the lilies self-seed and make offsets. If you peg a branch of the flowering currant to the soil it will root and form a new plant, while oceanspray and saskatoon will self-seed, and ferns pop up here and there, along with huckleberry, Oregon grape, arbutus trees, and many others: all this in keeping with the strategy of letting Nature play her part.

There are limits. I do occasionally need to pull out seedlings of sword fern, lady fern, arbutus, and saskatoon, and cut back straying roots of the Nootka rose or the native honeysuckle. And besides the bleeding heart and the redwood sorrel, some native

The western columbine, a common wildflower.

Simply scatter the seed and wait four years!

Pacific coast irises and blue camas.

plants can become rather too invasive—the foamflower (*Tiarella trifoliata*) for example, as well as over-aggressive shrubby thugs such as thimbleberry and salmonberry. I don't think the common form of the latter measures up to its botanical name, *Rubus spectabilis*, but the double form really *is* spectacular! It was discovered in 1961 in the wilderness of Washington State.

As for its provenance, Mother seemed a touch embarrassed. "Oh that," she said offhandedly. "That sport is the outcome of a bit of a fling I had in the Olympic Mountains a few hundred years ago. Ancient history."

It was clear the subject was closed.

9
The Lilies of the Field

WELL, I FELT I'D GONE a mile or two to satisfy Mother Nature's demands. And since she seemed to be in a more melodious mood, I asked, with the utmost deference, if she would, just possibly, tolerate some non-native plants in our garden.

"Mmmm . . . well maybe," she said. "But keep it simple."

"Simple?"

"Yes, simplicity pleases me. Grow things I have evolved and encouraged to grow in the wild elsewhere in the world. You know— what you call species, or perhaps wild variations or hybrids. At least avoid those things that have been put through generations of artificial crossbreeding—the fancy and fashionable—cultivars that hybridizers have created in an attempt to improve on *my* work. What a nerve! That's a form of evolution I call *unnatural* selection.

"Take that so-called tulip you have there. What a ghastly mess! Looks like a school of sharks. Did you actually *buy* that demented freak?"

And before I could answer, with one flick of a feather, Mother Nature reduced the clump to cinders.

"Now hold on, Mother," I objected. "That's going a bit far."

"Fiddleheads," she trilled. "That raggedy cripple would have died anyway. If you insist on growing tulips, at least grow something

A freak tulip summarily incinerated by Mother N.

that looks like a tulip. Stick to species. You'll find that's where beauty lies—in sheer simplicity."

Of course she was right again. In the wild, there are no cultivars—that is to say hybrids developed through intentional human activity. There are species: plants that have evolved to survive in their particular home and native land. There are variations and hybrids as well in the wild, but these too have passed the test of long-term survival. I have noticed that species—plants that exist in nature—often flourish in the garden, while their bastard offspring, the fancy cultivars of plant breeders, may not. Fashionable new varieties, this season's "hot plants," urged upon us in seductive catalogues, displayed in full bloom at nurseries, and touted by garden columnists, have probably been raised and cosseted in ideal greenhouse conditions. These, especially those most distant from their wild ancestors, are likely to be less robust when exposed to the real world of garden conditions and climate. Diminished in health and stature, less able to withstand pests and diseases than their forebears, they languish. In the wild too, Mother Nature, sooner or later, will abort a freak unless, through natural selection, it is chosen for some feature that gives it an edge in survival.

"Besides," added Mother, "you're aiming to develop what you think is the perfect garden aren't you? 'In imitation of Nature,' you said. If you really mean that, you have to go for plants found in the wild. Why not start with tulips? They're easy. They're eloquently simple, and they have history."

IN THE DAYS of dip pens, when I was an ink-stained schoolboy, a favourite experiment was to stand a pale-coloured tulip in an inkwell overnight. In the morning, the veins of the petals would be mapped out in black. It's a trick no doubt known to Dutch children of the 1630s, when tulip mania gripped the country and the most sought-after bulbs were those randomly flamed with colour on a white or yellow ground. We now know that this "breaking" is the work of a mosaic virus that's carried by aphids from plant to plant. In the seventeenth century, the cause was not understood. Nevertheless, breeders discovered that the effect could be induced by extracting sap from an infected plant and injecting it into another. The crosses with the most artful and delicate streaking were priced beyond gold. Literally. Homes were mortgaged to gamble on a single bulb, fortunes were made and fortunes lost in a single day.

The tulip gets its name from *tulipant*, a Turkish word for turban, which the flower is supposed to resemble. The wildlings, species from which the tens of thousands of garden cultivars bred over the past five hundred years have developed, are natives primarily of the Eastern Mediterranean. They are particularly associated with Turkey, which commanded much of that region in the glory days of the Ottoman Empire. It is believed that the introduction of the first tulip into Europe (*c.* 1555) can be credited to Ogier Ghiselin de Busbecq, a Renaissance man of great intellect, whose many accomplishments included collecting and writing about plants. His position as Ambassador of the Austrian Emperor to the Court of the Sultan, Suleiman the

Tulipa sprengeri, Sprenger's tulip.

Magnificent, in Constantinople, gave him access to the considerable variety of garden tulips already developed in Turkey. We don't know what varieties of tulip bulb he took home, but can make a guess from the characteristics valued by the Turks—aesthetics quite different from the familiar Dutch tulips of our time.

At the Ottoman court, the most favoured tulips had almond-shaped flowers, with narrow, dagger-shaped petals ending in long, needle-like points. Without these characteristics, a tulip was considered inferior. Paintings and ceramics of the Ottoman court of that era often illustrate tulips with six very long and very sharp (needle-pointed) petals.

The glowing, red-and-gold species *Tulipa sprengeri* has this favoured form, with six pointy petals. It is my prima donna assoluta, the first lady of the late spring garden, blooming in June. It's fertile, after the petals fall, forming shapely, three-chambered pods, packed with seeds like tiny wafers, round and flat, dispersed by wind, like most seeds of the lily family to which tulips belong. As are other wild tulips,

Sprenger's tulip with *Allium flavum*, yellow-flowered garlic.

this species is small, about ten centimetres tall: a delicate and discreet performer, quite unlike a chorus line of seventy-five-centimetre-tall modern tulip cultivars. I've not seen *T. sprengeri* for sale in garden centres, but it is listed in some mail-order bulb catalogues. Why buy it though? It's very easily grown from seed.

T. sprengeri was named for the brilliant, nineteenth-century German botanist, Carl Ludwig Sprenger, whose life had no sound. The American plant hunter David Fairchild noted that he was "very deaf" and observed, "Perhaps he loved plants so much because they spoke in colors, shapes, and scents."[1] That thought is arresting. It is a perceptive insight into the range of senses engaged by those who deeply appreciate the wonder of flower and foliage, as Sprenger surely did.

There's mystery surrounding this tulip. Supposedly, sometime before the First World War, a single bulb was found in a shipment to the Dutch bulb firm of Van Tubergen from their collector in Turkey. This specimen was traced to a mountainous area near the Black Sea coast of northern Turkey, a land of cold, dry winters and hot summers. Yet since that time, it has never been seen there! It has vanished in the wild, while still growing happily in a range of garden conditions. Are we to believe that the entire and widespread cultivation of Sprenger's tulip derives from a single bulb? Is it possible that the collector dug up a sport, a one-of-a-kind variation on the theme of tulip? Could it be that there never were others like it in the wild?

Regardless of its provenance, it is sheer, elegant simplicity in its foliage and proportions, brazen in colour, yet modest in size and form. If happy, it may, in a few years, establish colonies through self-seeding. To achieve this, patient and restrained minimalistic gardening is recommended. In other words, let Nature take her course. Let the fragile seedlings (which look like tiny, skinny threads of grass), find their feet: they're easily dislodged, so don't till the soil. Don't even scratch at the surface. I'm amazed to read that in some parts of the world this tulip may become invasive, to the point that in the 1950s, members of Britain's Alpine Garden Society were told not to send *T. sprengeri* to the seed exchange. True, it digs in deeply and can be difficult to remove from places where it's not welcome. But bring it on, I say. I can't imagine having too much of this tulip. It presents no threat to other plants. In any case, it's not likely to spread too freely in the Pacific Northwest; here, our wet winter dampens its enthusiasm for conquest.

Of course, a gardener choosing to grow Sprenger's tulip and other simple species cuts against the grain of popular taste for the showy hybrid cultivars. Whether Darwin, parrot, fringed, lily-flowered, peony-flowered, you-name-it flowered, these tulips come in every colour and mix of colours, even including green—every colour except blue. As with the rose, creation of a truly blue tulip has eluded hybridizers. But no matter—*dyed* blue tulips are on the market. It's back to the ink well.

Some statistics: The Netherlands, which provides more than ninety percent of the bulbs demanded around the world, produces three billion tulips a year. If planted ten centimetres apart, they would circle the Earth seven times. Twenty thousand people are employed in the Dutch bulb industry. A large farm may grow as many as sixty million bulbs. In May, viewed from the air, such a farm looks like a Mondrian painting, with huge rectangular blocks of brilliant, primary colours.

In 1945, in gratitude to Canada for giving wartime sanctuary to Princess Juliana and her children, the Dutch royal family sent a hundred thousand tulip bulbs to Ottawa. Interest on this gratitude continues in perpetuity, with an annual gift of twenty thousand bulbs. In 1953, this led to the foundation of the Canadian Tulip Festival, an annual event in the capital. Each fall, a million tulip bulbs are planted along the banks of the Rideau Canal, and in parks on both sides of the Ottawa River. A million planted in fall, a million blooming in May, soon thereafter dug up and replaced with a million fresh bulbs in fall. It's a Trooping the Colour that attracts tens of thousands of visitors.

What has this to do with simplicity? Well, nothing. It is the antithesis of simplicity, both in the labour required and the quantity of material consumed. On a much smaller scale, the municipal park or home gardener, wanting an eye-candy array of spring tulips, *en masse*, is also obliged to treat them as bedding plants, to be dug up after flowering and replaced with other temporary fillings, such as summer annuals, which, in turn, will be discarded when new tulips are set out in fall. Those handsome tulip cultivars, especially the fancier ones, will, generally speaking, bloom gloriously in the first spring after the bulbs are set out, sparsely (if at all) in the second, and are likely to give up or go blind in the third. On the other hand, the "botanical" tulips, as the trade calls those found in the wild—all simple, small, and uncluttered forms—will, generally speaking, recur every year and may slowly naturalize by seed or bulb offsets.

It's this simplicity, the quiet simplicity of the species tulips, that I love. Rather than seeking acclaim as star performers, they are happy to grow through and mingle in harmony at ground level with other spring plants. They belong in the chorus of the perfect garden. I like the plain, lance-shaped foliage that, once the flowers are finished, doesn't leave me with a heap of cabbagey leaves and stalks to clean up, as do the cultivars. I am pleased that these petite tulips are not flattened by wind and rain.

I've never seen a sign of botrytis or basal rot in any species tulip. Rodents do not eat them. Perhaps that's because rodents are alert to ground disturbance, and because these bulbs are never disturbed, their presence as a food source is never revealed.

There is of course no need to dig them up and I don't feed them. With no care or attention from me (other than lavish praise and affection), these little darlings can be counted upon to come back year after year, and in the process gently multiply. They demand nothing except to be left alone in a patch of sun.

In 1597, John Gerard, the Elizabethan physician and head gardener to the queen's principal advisor, Lord Burleigh, published his matchless herbal, *The Generall Historie of Plantes*. Therein, departing from his usual scientific rigour, he states his belief that Jesus was referring to the tulip when He said, "Consider the lilies of the field, how they grow: they toil not, neither do they spin. And yet I say unto you that Solomon in all his glory was not arrayed as one of these."[2] The reasons Gerard gives are these: "First, their shape: for their floures resemble Lillies; and in these places where our Saviour was conversant they grow wild in the fields. Secondly the infinite varietie of colour, . . . thirdly, the wondrous beautie and mixtures of their floures." He concludes: "This is my opinion, . . . which any may either approve of or gainsay, as he shall think good."[3]

I approve.

Today, all the fancy cultivars I ever planted, including those that Mother N. likened to "a school of sharks," have slowly and silently faded away. All that are left are species. I'm delighted to admire the showy tulips in other people's gardens and applaud the efforts they put in to thwart the rodents that dig them up, the winds that blast the flowers, and the slugs and snails that nip off the newly emerging shoots. It's a lot of work.

So I'll stick with the species. They belong in the carefree garden.

Wild Tulips (Species and Variations) in My Carefree Garden

T. turkestanica.

LEFT: *T. sylvestris.*
RIGHT: *T. batalinii.*

T. pulchella.

T. species.

The hoop petticoat daffodil.

10

The Simplicity of Species

THE WEB OF LIFE IS intricately woven. The separate threads, in the case of plant species, are often simple and undemanding. Such a thread is *Narcissus bulbocodium*, native to the south and west of France and the Iberian Peninsula. This is a tiny daffodil, resembling a hoop petticoat blowing in the wind.

I'm not sure if William Wordsworth was referring to *N. bulbocodium* when he wrote so lyrically of "a host of golden daffodils fluttering and dancing in the breeze." Probably not. But it's a fitting description of these elfin sweethearts. They also put me in mind of a host of festive fans at a football game. They all face the same way, staring at the sun.

I dearly love this little daffodil. In bloom, they're only about fifteen centimetres high and they're all flared trumpet with a vanishingly small perianth, which explains their nickname, hoop petticoat daffodil, for they do resemble in miniature the shapely underwear worn by ladies of fashion in the 1860s.

Unlike most of the commercially cultivated daffodils, their leaves are grass-like and don't leave a slug-ridden mess to clean up after the flowers have died. Most obligingly, they naturalize, spreading by seed. Most species do this. Most garden cultivars do not. Indeed, as with tulips, the showiest creations of the daffodil and narcissus breeders are likely to put out spectacular flowers the year after planted, go blind

A brass band of *Narcissus bulbocodium.*

in year two, and eventually disappear entirely. To ensure a recurring spectacle, they need to be purchased every year, planted in fall, dug up, and disposed of after blooming. Bedding plants again. Bedding plants are costly. Bedding plants require work. In my time, like most other gardeners, I have bought bedding plants galore from nurseries, or grown them myself from seed, planted them out in spring, watered and dead-headed them through summer, then thrown them on the compost pile in the fall cleanup. Now, I view reliance on bedding plants as a rather wasteful way to garden.

I do admire many of those fragrant, fancy forms of daffodil—the doubles, the pinks, the frillies, not to mention the double pink frillies, cultivars with seductive names such as 'Salome', 'Taffeta', 'Tahiti'—provided they're in other people's gardens. Not in ours, thank you.

Only those that bloom reliably year after year, demanding no attention whatsoever, will find a place in our garden. And having found a place, they're welcome to pop up wherever a seed finds a

Narcissus 'Tete-a-tete'.

spot that suits it. The hoop petticoat daffodil, with bulbs the size of a cherry pit, seems especially comfortable in the shallow, gritty soil of the rock garden. A self-seeder, it readily multiplies to form a brass band of blaring trumpets. It likes a dry summer. The only attention I give it is weeding out the fragile native grass that tries to masquerade as the daffodil's leaves.

Unfortunately you're not likely to find bulbs of this cheery little flower in your friendly neighbourhood garden centre, although some catalogues list it. I started it from seed and, as with the native bulbs, waited some years before seeing it in bloom.

As the spring crocuses are dying down, their place in our garden is taken by *Narcissus* 'Tete-a-tete', another unassuming miniature daffodil. By the end of March, the flowers open, often in pairs, two heads on a single stem having an intimate conversation, as it were—which accounts for the name. This is not a species, but a mixture of three, so not too far removed from the wild. It's sterile, so cannot be grown from seed, but will readily form clumps that can be divided any time

Rosa hugonis, Father Hugo's Rose.

after the foliage dies down and distributed informally around the garden, where, given a sunny spot, it will flower early and prolifically. Unless you live in an area with very cold winters or in the tropics, *anybody* can grow 'Tete-a-tete'. It's a perfect plant for the carefree garden. Our source is the local supermarket, which in late winter sells small plastic pots, with three or four bulbs in bud. We buy some, enjoy the blooms indoors, and then put the pots outside in a shed to dry. Through summer, the bulbs rest dormant until fall when I plant them in the garden, or in a container, where they flourish and multiply year after year. No fuss.

CAN A GARDEN be perfect without a rose?

The rose is the undoubted queen of the garden. From far-off times, it appears in painting and ceramics, and as architectural decoration. The rose is an ancient symbol of love and beauty. "My love is like a red, red rose," sang Robbie Burns. To the Greeks it represented Aphrodite, to the Romans, Venus. In Pharaonic Egypt, the rose was sacred to the top goddess, Isis. As a symbol, the five petals represented the five wounds of Christ for mediaeval Christians. The rose is the national flower of England and the floral emblem of the United States.

Its cultivation goes back at least to 500 BC in China and in Mediterranean countries. Hybridization began in earnest around two centuries ago and now, no fewer than six thousand five hundred different roses are available from some source somewhere in the world. Since there are only about a hundred species, almost all of these are the creations of rose breeders. Abetted by modern gene transfer technology, with replication by the thousand possible through plant tissue culture, this work proceeds apace—in particular, the quest for that ultimate horticultural horror, the blue rose.

It's not surprising then that in the garden, when confronted by roses, Mother Nature strives to topple the queen from her throne. She rolls out the heavy artillery. The list of pests includes aphids, spider mites, thrips, sawflies, caterpillars, Japanese beetles, cottony cushion

ABOVE AND OPPOSITE: *R. chinensis mutabilis*, the butterfly rose ... ever changing, as the name suggests.

scale, California red scale, rose scale, leaf-cutting bee, nematodes, rose chafer, and metallic flea-beetles. Deer and rabbits feed on the tender new shoots. Nature's arsenal of fungal diseases includes black spot, powdery mildew, downy mildew, rust, anthracnose, grey mould, verticillium wilt, sooty moulds, and canker. In case these don't do them in, roses are also prone to viral and bacterial diseases, including a new and fatal virus, the rose rosette virus, which infects only roses, as far as we know, and for which as yet there is no treatment.

Of course, a range of chemical weaponry has been mounted in defense of the garden rose, but crafty Ms. Nature is always one move ahead. Add to that the trend among eco-conscious jurisdictions to enact bylaws banning the use of chemical pesticides and fungicides for cosmetic reasons, and I detect a drift among gardeners to read the tea leaves and surrender, though some fight on, deploying aphid-eating ladybugs, insecticidal soap, neem oil, and other environmentally correct "organic" pest controls.

I love roses. Who doesn't? But it seems to me that a rose's resistance to disease weakens more or less in proportion to the distance of its relation to the original wild species. Therefore, having resolved to work with Nature and grow what she is most likely to tolerate, I have thrown out all the hybrid teas, and most of the shrubs, and narrowed the collection to a few disease-free climbers and—of course—species. They bloom just once in the year, but I don't care; in many, the glossy, ruby hips more than compensate. One of my favourites is *Rosa hugonis*, the Golden Rose of China or Father Hugo's Rose. It grows to a height of two-and-a-half metres, with graceful, arching branches, wreathed in masses of single, five-petalled, golden-yellow flowers in mid-May, one of the earliest roses to bloom. The flowers are followed by maroon-coloured hips. The leaves are pleasingly small, and bright green, turning yellow in fall before dropping. Even in winter, the bare framework has eye appeal. Few roses have year-round interest.

Father Hugo's Rose was raised in 1899 at Kew Gardens from seed sent from China by a missionary, Father Hugh Scanlan. Well over a century later, some of the original plants still grow at Kew. If it outgrows its space, chop it to the ground. It will come back. It is indestructible.

I find claims that a plant "will bloom all summer" are, more often than not, exaggerated. However, in the case of the butterfly rose, *Rosa chinensis mutabilis*, it holds true. In the Pacific Northwest, this antique rose will bloom from spring to frost, while in balmy climates such as southern California, it will bloom year round. With this rose, Mother Nature shows off her sense of fun, painting the single flowers in different colours: opening in sulphur yellow, changing through orange to a rich pink that gradually and finally darkens to mahogany rose red. Bright, silky flowers of all these colours will often be on display at the same time, looking as if a flock of multicoloured butterflies has alighted on the bush. The leaves too complement this mutability, changing from bronze in the new shoots to deep green in well-ripened branches.

The origins of this plant are a mystery. No doubt DNA testing might shed clues as to its ancestry, but I haven't heard that this has been done. It was originally sold under the fitting name 'Tipo Ideale' (ideal type). It is believed to have made its horticultural debut around 1896, when the botanist Henry Correvon found it growing on the estate of an Italian prince. It is not known whether the plant originated in China or was a hybrid born in the prince's garden. Whichever, it does appear to be an accidental, garden-originated hybrid, rather than a cultivar: a work of Mother Nature therefore, and accordingly not a likely host for plague and pestilence.

Among roses, *R. chinensis mutabilis* is a somewhat tender plant, rated hardiness zones 6 to 9. It will grow to about two metres tall and, while gardeners who like to be in charge recommend maintaining vigour and tidiness by cutting back the side shoots and removing about a quarter of the growth at the base, I'm inclined to let Nature take control, more or less. I rather like the rambling, unshaven look. It's more—well—*natural*.

I MAY SEEM to be unduly rigid in my insistence that, in my perfect garden, the only plants permitted are those that exist in Nature. Yes, in general, that is the goal, but not exclusively so. There are some plants that have been with me for a long time, showing their determination to stick around, surviving healthily, apparently happy in spite of receiving no care or attention other than occasional pruning. As I said, I have kept a few climbing roses. One of these is an old tea rose, *Rosa* 'Madame Grégoire Staechelin', introduced by a Spaniard in 1927 and therefore also named 'Spanish Beauty'. Her flowers are blousy, loose, and large. They hang from the branches in billowing masses, up to six metres above ground. Her petals are a warm pink, deepening in colour on the reverse. She's simply scrumptious.

I like to think that rose breeders name their most voluptuous creations after their most favoured, full-figured, female friends. Unwisely, I shared this thought with Mother Nature.

"Typical misogynistic objectification," she snapped.

11

The Twelfth Wedding Anniversary Flower

HYCROFT HOUSE IS AN EDWARDIAN mansion that stands on a walled, five-and-a-half-acre estate in Vancouver's wealthy Old Shaughnessy district. When this stately home was completed in 1911, the surrounding grounds included stables, a swimming pool, a coach house, and extensive manicured gardens. Hycroft became the centre of the Vancouver social scene and then, in 1942, the owner donated it all to the federal government for a dollar, deeding the estate to be used as a convalescent home for Canadian veterans.

For a time in the early 1960s, it was unoccupied and somewhat derelict. The building had been empty for two years, unheated, and without basic maintenance. The grass was knee high, bindweed and blackberry vines were growing through the walls. Raccoons had taken up residence.

Guided tours could be booked, an opportunity to explore Hycroft's shabby splendour: the enormous shower cages of brass and chrome, equipped with seven spray nozzles positioned to massage different body parts; the sweeping staircase, like a setting for *Gone with the Wind*; the cellars, with a honeycomb of holes in concrete walls for storing vintage wines; and the abandoned gardens, much overgrown.

There, among the few surviving plants, I found large clumps of

Paeonia veitchii responds well to neglect.

single, pink peonies. They must have been species but they had no message for me. This was my gaudy garden period (dinner plate dahlias) and I thought them dull.

They may have been *Paeonia veitchii*, which I came across forty years later, during a plant-hunting expedition with fellow plant people in the alpine meadows of Sichuan Province, China: a bank of pink peonies in full bloom. Over a century ago, seed was collected and introduced to English gardens by E.H. "Chinese" Wilson. He named it for the man who funded his expedition, the seedsman James Veitch. Blue-black seeds, the size of coffee beans, were scattered about. I collected a few, took them home, started them in a pot, and was pleased to see them germinate the following spring. Responding well to neglect, Veitch's peony, like most of its kin, is an ideal candidate for the perfect garden.

As I work within the frame of letting Nature show the way, in particular striving for simplicity, I could pen paeans of praise for peonies—species peonies that is. In deep, well-prepared, and

Paeonia mascula, the wild peony.

well-drained soil, most species are long-lived, reliably hardy, and fairly drought tolerant. They like elbow room, and resent disturbance—so much so that they may sulk and refuse to flower for two seasons or more if you dig them and divide them. Suits me: I have no inclination to move them. Many are fragrant. They are not usually on the deer or rabbit menu. Herbaceous species are beautiful through most of the year: from the fat, rosy shoots erupting in November as the old stems and leaves fall away, to the tender sprigs like pink asparagus in February, to the luxuriant spring foliage in green and coppery colours, to the simple, single flowers—big bowls of red, pink, yellow, or white, light and airy as a Bartók bagatelle—and finally, the red and black seedheads in late summer.

The peony, which is the twelfth wedding anniversary flower, is among the noblest and most historic of plants, with a three thousand-year tradition of cultivation for ornamental and medicinal purposes. The name *Paeonia* was bestowed by the long-lived Greek scholar Theophrastus (*c*.371–*c*.287 BC), often considered the father of botany. He named the plant for Paeon, in Greek mythology the physician who served the Olympian gods, healing their wounds in battle. Paeon was a student of Asclepius, the Greek god of medicine and healing. His mentor became murderously jealous of his protégé's healing abilities, but Paeon was saved by Zeus, who turned him into a flower. The peony therefore is believed to have healing qualities.

The dried, pulverized roots and the bark of the tree peony have been used in herbal medicine to treat high blood sugar, blood clots, and stomach pain. Peony is also an old herbal remedy for "female complaints." For women, further benefits were found in its effectiveness in steadying the nerves, while men have enjoyed its rewards for an overall feeling of well-being. Here you have the traditional sexist view of the strong, enduringly steady man, enjoying a well-deserved buzz of hearty good feeling, while little wifey needs something to control her hysteria. (See also hellebores in the following chapter.)

Peony species grow in our garden as if they liked growing. All were easily grown from seed. It will take four years, possibly more, for the seedling to mature and flower. The rewards are worth the wait.

Herbaceous *Paeonia mascula*, the wild peony, is the first to flower. It's native to Mediterranean islands and has also naturalized on two tiny limestone islets in Britain's Bristol Channel: Steep Holm and Flat Holm. It settles down happily in our Mediterranean summers. The wild peony unfurls in spring, flaunting utterly simple and utterly gorgeous big red blooms. They last merely a week, before slowly fading to pink, then white before the petals drop. It's self-fertile and hermaphroditic, having both male (red) and female (black) fruit, held round and shiny like M&Ms in the ripe seed pod, itself a thing of remarkable beauty.

Now what fancy double peony cultivar will do *that* for you?

Even in mid-winter, when these and other herbaceous species start to sprout, the tender new shoots are colourful and succulent—attractively juicy to slugs. These must be kept at bay.

As the wild peony fades to white, the Japanese woodland peony, *P. obovata alba*, unfurls its petals; the flowers are held above red-stemmed foliage, with young leaves also faintly veined in red. A friend recently said to Rosemary and me, "Gardening is all about texture and foliage and structure. Flowers are just the icing on the cake." Well, I've come to agree with that, but in this case—some icing! The flower is a chalice of purest white, holding in its centre a wad of purple filaments topped with yellow anthers. Among all peony species, this is my favourite. *P. obovata* was used by the Ainu people of Japan as a painkiller. Simply looking at the white form in bloom well might put pain out of mind. And again, there are showy seeds, though here the male and female develop in separate capsules.

Paeonia mlokosewitschii grows in the Caucasus Mountains and is named for a Polish botanist with an equally unpronounceable name, Ludwik Mlokosiewicz, who discovered it in 1897. It is known to intimate friends (among whom I count myself), as Molly-the-witch. In the wild, it is the only yellow herbaceous peony and another distinctly beautiful and singularly simple species.

Molly is rather promiscuous, inclined in the garden to cross with other species. Accordingly, you may start seed and wait for years for her

The wild peony seedhead, a bonus for growing fertile species.

to bloom, only to discover you have pink. The real thing is invariably butter yellow.

TREE PEONIES—WHICH are not trees but deciduous woody shrubs—have been grown in China as a medicinal plant for two thousand years. There too, new cultivars have been created over a period of at least ten centuries. In the seventh century, cultivated plants in the Imperial Gardens were considered so valuable that the emperor issued an edict giving them his personal protection. Eventually, in 1903, the charismatic and powerful dowager empress Cixi named the tree peony the national flower of China. When Mao's joy-killing Cultural Revolution tried to ban ornamental tree peony cultivation, the Chinese continued to grow them under the guise of medicinal plants. Today, the tree peony is as popular as ever. Though not restored to the throne of national flower on the mainland (the Nationalist Chinese took that symbol with them to Taiwan), it's considered the perfect Chinese New Year present, symbolizing prosperity, good fortune, and love.

P. mascula in winter, a delicacy for slugs.

The sublime Japanese woodland peony. Some icing!

The golden peony, familiarly known as Molly-the-witch.

P. mlokosewitschii is the only yellow herbaceous peony species.

P. rockii var., named for the botanist Joseph Rock.

Of course, I stand in awe of the scores of aristocratic tree peony cultivars, mainly derivations of the Chinese species *P. suffruticosa* and *P. rockii*, with their splendid blooms up to eighteen centimetres across. I respect the diligence of peony specialists who will go so far as to construct little roofs, supported on bamboo canes, to protect the fragile blooms from inclement weather. However, in keeping with Mother Nature's instructions, I stick with simplicity, growing species that are relatively humble in flower but will not be slapped about and broken in rain.

Among them is *P. lutea*, the classic Tibetan tree peony, rare in gardens, although obligingly undemanding and very easy to grow from shiny black seeds the size of cocktail olives. It forms a handsome woody shrub up to two metres in height, and will self-seed. In spring, clusters of fresh leaves emerge from terminal buds in shades of green and mahogany bronze to salute the lengthening days, a feature just as beautiful as the yellow double flowers with orange centres in June. If well placed, the large, bright green, heavily dissected leaves stand in contrast, yet in harmony, with shrubby companions—most notably Father Hugo's Rose.

P. lutea's close kin, the Victorian tree peony, *P. delavayi*, is named for Jean Marie Delavay, who served Missions Etrangères de Paris in Guandong and Yunnan provinces of China from 1867 until his death in 1895. Aside from carrying out the duties of his ministry, Delavay was a plant hunter extraordinaire. Over the years he sent more than two hundred thousand herbarium specimens to the Museum of Natural History in Paris, among them fifteen hundred new species.

Père Delavay was, according to E.H.M. Cox, exceedingly thorough and meticulous in his method. "Near his residence was a mountain called Tsemei-shan, which he called at the same time his garden and the Mont Blanc of Yunnan. This he climbed from every angle and at every season of the year, no fewer than sixty times . . ."[1] Moreover, he travelled on foot and alone, unlike other great plant hunters of the late nineteenth and early twentieth centuries, who usually engaged a large retinue of porters, assistants, guides, cooks, interpreters, with a train of pack horses and mules to carry the associated baggage and supplies.

I would have liked to meet this holy man.

The tree peony he found, *P. delavayi*, is another large and hardy deciduous shrub, endemic to China. The young leaves are reddish-bronze, changing within weeks to bright green. It flowers in June, with deep-red blooms. Fragrant too—sweetly fragrant the catalogues will say, though some might disagree. The scent is musky, spicy, sophisticated—an acquired taste.

In all, there are about thirty-three peony species. Whether tree or herbaceous, at a specialized nursery these noble plants in flowering size may cost you a hundred dollars. You can grow them from seed for free. I have collected seeds from other gardeners and from the seed exchanges of societies such as the Alpine Garden Club of British Columbia, which is worth joining for the seed exchange alone.

The peony represents wealth and honour. Peonies symbolize romance and prosperity and are regarded as an omen of good fortune and the promise of a long and happy marriage.

For the gardener willing to let Nature have it her way, peony species are the embodiment of simplicity.

Deciduous *P. lutea*, and its tender, fresh leaves in spring.

P. delavayi, the Victorian tree peony.

12

It Isn't Easy Being Green

MOTHER NATURE WAS WEARING HER black-crested jay outfit, preening her cobalt blue feathers in our birdbath. "Do me a favour," I said. "Please tell your shiny corvid cousins, the crows, to stop washing chicken bones and bits of hotdog in your bathwater. Every morning I have to scrub it clean."

"Tell 'em yourself. Crows will be crows, and crows have no manners at all."

She continued her toilette, ignoring me, repeatedly plunging her head into her bath, then wielding her long black beak to wash dirt from her body, and to snatch and swallow a flea that had foolishly burrowed under a wing. I waited, while she carefully picked through her feathers, aligning them just so, before applying a dab of oil from the supply she carried under her tail. Finally, she checked her appearance in the mirror surface of the water, gave her feathers one last shake, and turned to me.

"Surprise, surprise, it looks like you've got the message. If you want to create what you call your perfect garden you have to stick close to me. If you want to be close to me you have to keep it simple. Mother Nature is pleased with simplicity. Accordingly, I am pleased with you."

I was gobsmacked. Speechless. Not that Mother would have been interested in any remark from me. As always, she had her own agenda. "And now, you must grow hellebores," she declared.

"Really? To me a hellebore is just that—a hell of a bore."

Mother sighed. "There you go again, a predictably facile remark. You're looking for simplicity aren't you? 'Easy care,' you say? Plants that pretty well take care of themselves, yet are among the most beautiful I have evolved? Well, the hellebore's your man."

"Whatever you say. Still, they certainly don't pump my nads."

Stubborn as ever, Ms. Bossy-Boots ignored my vulgarity. "I'll keep it simple, stupid, so you can understand. Consider the equation $N \times L = S$, where N represents the degree of a plant's tolerance of neglect, measured on a scale of one to ten, while L is a measure of its loveliness, also measured on a scale of one to ten. Are you with me? The multiple of the two, S, is the *coefficient of simplicity*. That's the measure of a plant's suitability for a creaky and increasingly decrepit gardener, such as you, seeking the greatest possible satisfaction for the least possible effort. Look no further than hellebores."

I told you: Nature can do math. I rolled my eyes. Frankly, I was finding her pedantic and condescending, but held my tongue.

"Furthermore," said Mother, "in this case—but mind you only in this case—I'm going to set aside my insistence that you stick to species, because I have to concede that hellebore breeders, like my dear old friend Helen Ballard, have mostly demonstrated excellent taste and produced hybrids that retain and even enhance the classic charms of the species. Few silly frillies or freaks."

Here's a break, I thought. We're getting a touch closer to that spirit of cooperation I had in mind from the start. "Okay," I said. "Bring 'em on."

Of course, you don't have to be an Einstein to figure out that hellebores *do* have a very high coefficient of simplicity. They're frost hardy, usually unattractive to bugs (except for slugs) and generally free of plague (except for black spot). Provided they are sited in moist, well-drained soil, not in full sun, hellebores are long-lived—earning a nine on the N scale. As for the L factor, hellebores *are* lovely. They're

Helleborus x hybridus, Lenten roses.

in bloom with the snowdrops when little else is on display, brightening the dismal months with flowers that last for an exceptionally long time. Moreover, the foliage is evergreen and, later in the year, will make a pleasing composition along with the foliage of other plants, such as epimediums, hostas, and ferns. No doubt a more diligent caretaker than I might get better performance with greater attention to watering in periods of drought and mulching in winter with organic compost, as well as treating them to an annual sprinkling of slow-release fertilizer, but I don't seem to get around to such tender loving care. I'm leaving that to Nature.

Botanically speaking, too, the hellebore is sheer simplicity. It belongs to the ranunculus family, a very diverse group that includes such unlikely cousins as buttercups, aconites, clematis, and columbines. In plant evolution this is an ancient and primitive family. One of its traits is the absence of the calyx, the sheath that encloses the bud in most flowers. So what we think we see on the hellebore in bloom—five large, overlapping petals—are actually coloured, translucent *sepals*.

These normally form the green outer covering of a flower, protecting the more delicate inner parts. This is why hellebore flowers last so long, up to two months and even more where spring is long and cool, persisting prettily until the seed pods are ripe and then slowly fading to a washed-out green or beige. As for petals, they're there in miniature, surrounding the naughty bits. They've been modified into nectaries, up to thirty-two of them, small, stunted, tubular, and flattened, usually but not always green, regardless of the colour of the flower, part of the delicate charm of the hellebore.

THERE ARE FEW plants of greater antiquity or more surrounded by legend and superstition than the Christmas rose, the black hellebore, *Helleborus niger*. It's also known as Christ's Herb because "it flowerith about the birth of our Lord." For centuries, it was planted close to cottage doors in the belief it would prevent evil spirits from crossing the threshold. And just in case they did, for good measure leaves and flowers were scattered about the house as well. It is native to the mountainous regions of Central and Southern Europe, Greece, and Turkey.

In the Christian tradition, there's a legend about the origins of the Christmas rose. A poor young shepherd girl called Madelon wanted to come and worship the infant Christ. Seeing the splendid gifts of the three kings—gold, frankincense, and myrrh—Madelon despaired that she had nothing to offer. Instead, she searched the snow-covered land for a flower to present. But the winter was bleak and the wind bitter, and no flower was to be found. Distraught, the child wept. And miraculously, as her tears fell, each was transformed into a beautiful flower, with white petals, tinged with pink. So Madelon gathered an armful and took them to the stable in Bethlehem, and was thrilled when the Babe turned from the gifts of the wise men and instead put out a tiny hand to touch her bouquet.

MY FATHER WAS a British naval officer. He sailed the seven seas for thirty years and fought in both world wars, in the service of two

The hellebore: sheer simplicity, delicate charm.

H. niger, the Christmas rose.

Georges and one inconsequential stopgap. When not at sea, he loved to garden and in his last years spent every spare daylight moment working among his flowers and vegetables, especially vegetables. In his memory, "while the light lasts" became a standard family excuse even years after he died, for he would often hurry through his meal and leave the table, saying he must do this or that outside "while the light lasts." My sister and I were expected to do the dishes.

One of my jobs in the garden, as he turned the soil and shook out the heavy clumps with a digging fork, was to trail behind and pick up the weeds. Much as I loved my father, if the seed of an avid gardener was within me at that time, this dreary assignment might have killed it. But my mother, who (as in most well-regulated families) was in charge of the flower department, kept it alive by giving me my own small patch where I would grow, from seed, easy things such as mustard, cress, calendulas, and sweet peas.

Around St. Patrick's Day, in the years after the war, when I was a lad and a very green gardener, my father would bundle the family into our pre-war Hillman Minx and motor clear across Suffolk to visit his cousin. The purpose of this annual pilgrimage was to see the green roses, grown by the cousin in his small garden. There was, as I recall, a bush growing by the front gate. I remember a sense of disappointment that the flowers were not as green as I expected. They were sort of green, but not emerald green, not grass green. They were more or less yellowy green. Nevertheless, to my trusting eyes the bush was without doubt a rose. After all, my father said so. Was he serious? Was he kidding? I'll never know.

I do know now that the plant we drove across the county to see was *not* a rose. There are no green roses. Nor, in that part of the world, do roses flower in March. It was a hellebore, *Helleborus argutifolius*, once known as *H. corsicus*, the Corsican hellebore, and in cultivation for at least five hundred years. This is the largest and hardiest of the tribe. In the Pacific Northwest it flourishes, evergreen, apparently happy in both sun and dappled shade: a well-behaved, clump-forming plant, difficult to divide but spreading its seed promiscuously.

In plant identification, botanical Latin is useful because the species name usually gives a clue to the appearance of the plant or some part thereof: its size, smell, or colour, where it's from, who found it. Thus, *corsicus* tells us where this hellebore originated: the Mediterranean islands of Corsica and Sardinia. The name was good for a hundred and fifty years, until the members of the International Commission for the Nomenclature of Cultivated Plants, sticklers for proper taxonomic procedure, changed it to *Helleborus argutifolius* on the grounds that when the species name *corsicus* first appeared on a list in 1813, it was without illustration or botanical description. On the other hand *argutifolius*, listed in 1824, eleven years later, was properly registered with illustration and description. Accordingly, this is the name we're obliged to use, even though *corsicus* had served as the official scientific name for most of the nineteenth and twentieth centuries!

I regret that the members of the committee were, in this case, unbending on the strictest application of the rules. I'm also unable

The Corsican hellebore: not a green rose.

to grasp the logic of *argutifolius*. The adjective (*argutus*) describes the leaf (*folius*). But to my eye, the leaf is not noticeably wise, witty, cunning, acute, eloquent, or even particularly expressive—which are among the several translations of *argutus* I've been able to dig up.

EACH YEAR, MEMBERS of the Perennial Plant Association from across North America vote to select a perennial with good performance over a wide range of climates. The 2005 winner was the Lenten rose, a hellebore.

To which I have to say, "You've come a long way, baby." For this plant, through much of the twentieth century, was valued by few gardeners. The Lenten rose was, by and large, a drab and dreary, dull-purple, dogshit-spattered, border plant, seen mainly in massed formations in municipal parks. Unloved and unwanted. Several famous garden books entirely omit any reference to hellebores of any kind:

- Eleanor Perenyi gives no thought to hellebores in her *Green Thoughts*;
- Russell Page's *Education of a Gardener* excludes any education about hellebores;
- The hellebore is entirely unessential for Henry Mitchell in *The Essential Earthman*;
- No growing space is reserved for hellebores in Thalassa Cruso's classic *Making Things Grow Outdoors*.

In fact, with the exception of one species, the genus was consigned to oblivion for decades. Go back to the beginning of the last century, though, and things look a little brighter. Gertrude Jekyll was a fan. She made good use of red, white, and purple Lenten roses in her landscapes. But by mid-century the plant was out of fashion. Not entirely ignored: a few sang its praises, among them Christopher Lloyd in Britain and Katherine White in the United States. Most of the attention, however, was paid to the Christmas rose, which never lost its popularity. Even in Britain, where in two world wars gardens everywhere were converted to vegetable growing, there was usually a Christmas rose tucked beneath a shrub.

The Lenten rose wears coats of many colours. It's listed in some catalogues as *Helleborus orientalis* hybrids, but is now more commonly named *Helleborus x hybridus*, for the DNA of as many as ten different species is woven through this plant in various quantities and combinations. In the white, *H. orientalis* is dominant, with other orientalis subspecies introducing spots and red tints. *H. odorus* accounts for the yellow and also plays a part in the greens, along with *H. cyclophyllus*. Breeders are striving to produce a real butter yellow and one day will. Meantime, pale yellow is as good as it gets. The rich purple and slate-black flowers take their colour from *H. torquatus* and *H. purpurascens*.

If there's a single hellebore breeder who can be credited with rescuing the Lenten rose from neglect and obscurity and projecting it onto the world stage as a superstar of the late twentieth century, still reigning in the twenty-first, that would be Helen Ballard. Her incomparable work at her garden and nursery in England set a standard of excellence perhaps still unmatched. She was in her fifties when she took on the Lenten rose in 1961. She had the field to herself in the nursery trade. There was scant demand from gardeners for the plant, but she appreciated its qualities and the potential of an intensive breeding program. She was so taken with hellebores that she learned German in order to understand texts about the genus written in that language. She started with just four Lenten roses, two whites and two reds, and continued her work, crossing and recrossing obsessively into old age, when she could be found driving an electric mobility scooter between the furrows of her hellebore field.

Helen Ballard died in 1995, aged eighty-six, but some years earlier, to ensure that her work would endure, she gave her entire stock to Gisela Schmiemann in Cologne, who indeed continued to use the Ballard plants and had a mail-order business distributing hellebore

H. argutifolius, the largest of the hellebore tribe.

A particularly fine Lenten rose, plant of the year in 2005.

seed worldwide. She also wrote a book about her mentor and her remarkable hellebore-breeding achievements.[1]

It is impossible to sort out the provenance of the great variety of Lenten roses we have in our gardens, but it's highly likely that many of them contain a bit of Helen Ballard's breeding program. In Europe and America, other hellebore specialists have built on her work, most notably in England where John Massey's Ashwood Garden Hybrids are internationally celebrated as simply the best strain of Lenten roses available today.

But when all is said and done, for sheer simplicity, I love the quiet humility of the species such as *H. dumetorum*, so bashful that you have to play hide and seek with it before finding the waxy green flowers among the green leaves. I love it because, as Kermit the frog sings: "... green's the colour of Spring. And green can be cool and friendly-like. And green can be big like an ocean, or important like a mountain, or tall like a tree. When green is all there is to be ... I think it's what I want to be."[2]

A fine specimen in Kathy Leishman's garden.

A freckled white form.

'Betty Ranicar' was first found in a garden in Tasmania.

A slate-coloured edition of *H x hybridus*.

A beautiful, informal bouquet of Lenten roses in Pam Frost's garden.

IN MY PURSUIT of the perfect garden, I particularly like to include plants with history, such as the peony. But unlike the peony, with its symbolism of riches, happiness, and so forth, the hellebore is an Old World plant having a long history of sinister associations with demons and possession, witchcraft and evil spells: a baneful plant.

Helleborus niger, the Christmas rose, is called the black hellebore because "its heart or root is black while its face shines with a blazing white innocence."[3] Among the great plant hunters of a century ago, there is no more expressive a writer than Reginald Farrer, and in those words he perfectly portrays the shining allure of the flower, hiding a black heart that harbours one of Nature's death-dealing plant poisons.

The genus has a dark history of deadly pharmaceutical experiment. In the first recorded instance of chemical warfare, during the siege of Kirrha in 585 BC, hellebore was reportedly used by the besiegers to poison the city's water supply. The defenders were thus so weakened by diarrhea that they were unable to repel the final assault and conquest.

Bashful *Helleborus dumetorum*, hiding its green flowers.

Another name for the black hellebore is melampode, after the shepherd Melampus who, according to Greek tradition, moonlighting as a soothsayer and physician around 1400 BC, supposedly cured his king's daughters of melancholy by dosing them with the milk of goats that had grazed on the black hellebore. In some versions he fed them the herb itself.

A warning of the poisonous nature of hellebore is embedded in its name, which comes from two Greek words: *elein*, meaning to injure or harm and *bora*, meaning food. Harmful food. The degree of damage depends on how much you ingest and, like so many poisons, such as digitalis and belladonna, it has had therapeutic applications.

Knowledge of the powerful toxicity of the hellebore and its corresponding medicinal misuse goes back to ancient times. For example, writing in the first century, the Roman naturalist and historian Pliny the Elder (he who died at Pompeii following the eruption of Vesuvius) recommends the herb "to purge the brain in order to make it better for serious study." Naturally, it was the women who were perceived to have the greater need for brain purging and besides that, it was widely used as an emmenagogue: that is, a treatment to bring on menstruation, to bring about abortion. The Greek physician Dioscorides, in *De Materia Medica*, listed hellebore as a component of abortion wine. And Hippocrates, in *Diseases of Women*, describes a drink—a cocktail made of hellebore, myrrh, spikenard, pine resin, and saltpetre—to bring about abortion. Hippocrates compares the effects of a dose of hellebore to hysterical suffocation—in women of course. In fact, as you might expect in a society run by men, it was women who were most frequently dosed with the plant.

However, ladies, be of good cheer. Men were also beneficiaries of this dicey medication. As recently as a century ago, dried and pulverized hellebore roots, mixed with other herbs, were offered in homeopathic remedies to cure, among other things, incontinence and snoring. Try that on your old man. But take care: a rather too permanent cure may occur, as recounted in the following cautionary tale:

> A greedy old man from Peru,
> Dipped a finger in hellebore stew.
> "Madre Dios," he cried,
> As he horribly died,
> "I thought it was chocolate fondue."

HELLEBORUS FOETIDUS IS one of the most widespread of the genus. Its common name, stinking hellebore, is undeserved. I find its musky scent quite agreeable, though certainly unusual. The whole plant is fragrant, infused with aromatic oil, which may leave its scent on your hand if you merely brush the leaves. The part that really is foul-smelling is the root, they say, but I've not yet dug one up to confirm this. Needless to say, nurseries don't list "stinking" hellebore. It won't sell. They call it "bear's foot," one of several mediaeval names.

In 1597, John Gerard was probably referring to bear's foot when he wrote that "a purgation of Hellebor is good for mad and furious men, for dull and heavy persons, and briefly, for all those that are

H. lividus, the blue-grey hellebore, native to Majorca.

The stinking hellebore, also known as dungwort or bear's foot.

troubled with blacke choler and molested with melancholy."[4] The belief in the plant's efficacy as a cure for mania persisted throughout the seventeenth century and who knows—maybe it did the trick. However, many poisonous narcotics have a tranquilizing effect in small doses and it's likely that hellebore did not so much cleanse minds as drug them into submission.

In mediaeval times, bear's foot was used for repelling witches and evil spirits, and breaking spells and enchantments. It was also commonly used in the veterinary practice of the day; if a cow fell sick, whether through poison or evil spells, the practice was to bore a hole through the wretched animal's ear and insert a piece of the root, like the latest thing in organic jewellery. This was removed the following day, by which time the trouble was supposed to be cured.

In the eighteenth century *H. foetidus* was extolled as a vermifuge—a treatment for worms, especially in children. A contemporary observer noted, "Where it kills not the patient, it will certainly kill the worms; but the worst of it is, it will sometimes kill both."[5]

In the nineteenth century, Sir Robert Christison, a physician and toxicologist who was Queen Victoria's personal doctor at Balmoral, did not hesitate to risk his own life ingesting potentially lethal toxins while gathering data for his treatise on poisons, published in 1829. Probably his description of the consequences of eating hellebore is, up to a point, based on his own experience.

"I have known severe griping produced by merely tasting the fresh root in January. Poisonous doses of hellebore occasion in man singing in the ears, vertigo, stupor, thirst, with a feeling of suffocation, swelling of the tongue and throat, emesis and catharsis, slowing of the pulse, and finally collapse and death from cardiac paralysis. Inspection after death reveals much inflammation of the stomach and intestines, more especially the rectum."[6]

Hellebore was a minor ingredient in Beecham's Pills, invented by Thomas Beecham (grandfather of the great English conductor Sir Thomas Beecham). From the middle nineteenth century, this over-the-counter cure-all was an extremely popular remedy in Western

Double-flowering variations of the Lenten rose are sought after. I prefer the simplicity of the singles.

Europe for constipation and tummy aches. Beecham's Pills could still be found on drugstore counters until 1998 when this proprietary medicine was finally withdrawn.

Today, hellebore is still used in homeopathic medicine. But I don't plan to chance it, lest I should suffer the pain of a certain young lady from Spain,

who was dreadfully sick on a train;

and again, and again,

and again, and again,

and again and a g a i n and *a g a iii nnnn.*

13
Serendipity

S ERENDIPITY IS A TUNEFUL WORD. Strictly speaking, it means the accident of finding something good and useful while not specifically searching for it. In the history of science, serendipity has played a very important part. A well-known example happened on September 3, 1928, when the Scottish biologist Alexander Fleming, at work in his laboratory, noticed that a culture of the bacteria *Staphylococcus* had become contaminated with fungi, and the mould was destroying the microbes. This led to the development of penicillin and other antibiotics, and the saving of countless lives. More loosely, serendipity describes the occurrence of happy accidents, of things that come about by chance.

I have lately recognized that serendipity plays a leading role in developing the carefree garden, and therefore have wholeheartedly embraced the value of serendipitous happenings. What's more, I've realized that these are a likely outcome of simplicity. Let the free-seeders seed freely. Let the spreaders spread, the runners run, the creepers creep. Let happy accidents abound. If Mother Nature finds a plant unsuited, let her summon pests or diseases or frost or heat to put it out of its misery. Let her do the work and make many of the decisions.

While I've only lately put a label on it, I realize that I have followed this strategy of leaving much to chance for years. For example, I have

Cyclamen coum in winter: serendipitous cross-pollination creates different leaf patterns and colours.

gratefully exploited the fact that cyclamen recruit ants to look after the dispersal of their seed, which might otherwise simply fall at the feet of the mother plant and never claim new territory. The plants offer a reward, of course: a tempting treat for the scatter-footed scavengers. The seeds are coated with a sticky, sugary delicacy. Ants are attracted, carry off the prize, lick it like a lollipop, and dump the seed undamaged. This mutually beneficial relationship is known as "myrmecochory" and has evolved between ants and as many as three thousand plants all over the world. An exquisite instance of "You scratch my back, I'll scratch yours."

Anyway, as a result of myrmecochory, with no assistance from me, tiny cyclamen plants pop up in surprising places. They make themselves at home in rocky crevices or a gravel pathway. They crowd the feet of a climbing rose and a competing twining honeysuckle. Seed may fetch up by chance in the compost heap, and from there germinate who can say where. This exuberant colonization is undertaken by those of the wild cyclamen that are hardy enough to withstand a touch of Pacific Northwest frost, such as *CC. hederifolium, mirabile,*

C. coum, from seed dropped by ants in nooks and crannies.

cilicium, purpurascens, and *graecum*, species that flower in summer and well into October, and the winter- and spring-flowering species, CC. *coum, libanoticum*, and *repandum*.

A TUBER OF the ivy-leaved cyclamen (*C. hederifolium*), can grow to the size and shape of a Frisbee. From its surface, starting in August, pink, red, or white flowers spring from the bare earth. The leaves follow, weaving marbled mosaics that hug the ground throughout the winter, providing a colourful mat at a time of year when all around is bare. In gardens, there's much serendipitous hybridizing among these merrymakers, so that, depending on the parents, the variations of leaf form, patterns, and colour are infinite within the range of green and grey, pewter and silver. In late spring, most vanish entirely, quietly waiting for shorter, cooler nights. Being natives of Mediterranean lands, they conserve their strength and go dormant, resting through hot, dry summers, a habit that fits the climate of the Pacific Northwest.

The ancient, colloquial name for cyclamen is sowbread or, in the fancier shops, *panis porcinus*, because the tubers were thought to be uprooted and eaten by pigs. Perhaps the pigs, animals noted for their intelligence, were on to something. For, as the English herbalist, John

Wonders Never Cease

The development and distribution of cyclamen seed is, I think, an exquisite instance of evolutionary cunning. The five-petalled flowers are held atop a leafless stem. The petals fall, exposing an immature seed pod. Thereupon the stem winds itself into a coil, tightly hugging the seed pod at ground level, and thus giving it protection from predators and stormy weather. It's easy to imagine that the plant has a mothering instinct.

With further protection from the emerging leaves, the seed pod expands, eventually ripening as a capsule about the size of a pea containing several sugary seeds. At this stage, the pod splits and the ants are summoned. Dinner is served.

Flowering in fall, the ivy-leaved cyclamen serendipitously spreads.

Gerard related: "[Sowbread] being beaten and made up into little cakes, is reported to be a good amorous medicine to make one in love, if it be inwardly taken."[1] Which may explain Miss Piggy's prowess in matters of the heart: "Moi has always possessed a charm that is lethal to men."

IN EARLY SPRING, as the flowers of the winter-blooming cyclamen begin to fade, a pink tide of squill (*Scilla bifolia* var. *rosea*) floods the garden, to be followed immediately by the rather more attractive, blue Siberian squill (*S. siberica*). Both have the agreeable habit of self-propagating promiscuously in sun or light shade and well-drained soil, living long and trouble-free lives. They'll happily spread around the base of deciduous trees and shrubs and, like the cyclamen, find a home in rock crevices and crannies, an exemplary instance of simplicity and serendipity in the garden. *Un*like the cyclamen though, squills do not engage ants to scatter their seed and are more likely to form dense mats of blue. When the seed is ripe and ready to fall, a minute or two spent with a lawn rake (very gently) will help spread the colony.

Self-scattering bulbs of blue Siberian squill.

Viola odorata, the sweet English violet.

Scilla siberica is not, as you might assume, from Siberia, but rather from Turkey and the neighbouring Caucasus. However, the rules of botanical naming do not allow a scientific name to be changed simply because it is potentially misleading.

Then greet the sweet violet, the English violet (*Viola odorata*), for some an unwelcome guest in a lawn, a weed. Years ago, I imported a piece from the much-loved English garden of a much-loved aunt and tucked it into bed in our garden, at the foot of a rhododendron. It took stock of its new home and decided to stay. Serendipity did the rest.

I don't have a lawn and, for me, this free-spreading, self-seeding blue poppet is now a welcome guest almost anywhere in the garden it chooses to call home. In shady areas, where the soil is poor and root-riddled, where the going is tough, the sweet violet gets going, happy to muck in with other durable ground covers such as bugle-weed (*Ajuga*), the purple primrose 'Wanda', and the aggressive, pink-flowered bigroot cranesbill (*Geranium macrorrhizum*). Other weeds don't get a look in.

Aside from its unique fragrance (only a violet smells like a violet), *Viola odorata* owns a centuries-long association with literature and

Be Warned of a Woodland Weed

However desirable they may be in gardens, hardy cyclamen are under suspicion as a potential invasive usurper, elbowing out native plants in deciduous woodlands, especially the unique Garry oak meadows of southern Vancouver Island. Here's a warning from the Garry Oak Ecosystems Recovery Team:

"As a Mediterranean [genus], cyclamen, and *C. hederifolium* in particular, are well adapted to Garry oak woodland conditions. A prolific seed producer prized by gardeners as a naturalizing ground cover, the disc-shaped tubers can exceed twenty-five centimetres in diameter, and have been observed in some locations to crowd out native plants. Patches of cyclamen in the Victoria area appear to be expanding more rapidly than in the past."[2]

symbolism. The poets called upon it: "... the violet embroidered vale" (Milton); "... by ashen roots the violets blow" (Tennyson); "A violet by a mossy stone ..." (Wordsworth, from a ballad to the grace and beauty of his Lucy, an idealized woman who lived only in the lonely poet's imagination). Shakespeare's plays are strewn with violets, their symbolism of love and fidelity, their fragrance: "I think the king is but a man, as I am. The violet smells to him as it doth to me." (Indeed it doth, for this line is spoken by King Henry V himself, as he goes in disguise among his men on the eve of the Battle of Agincourt.)

The sweet violet often hides its face among the heart-shaped foliage, which is why shy people may be referred to as "shrinking violets." In the Middle Ages, the flower was a symbol for modesty and humility, and was associated with the demure Virgin Mary. Its habit of spreading in all directions, sending out shoots and runners that set up new plants wherever they touch the ground, was acclaimed as emblematic of the spread of Christianity.

In majestic Elizabethan prose, John Gerard painted the virtues of the garden violet, giving them "a great prerogative" above other flowers "... not only because the mind conceiveth a certain pleasure and recreation by smelling and handling these most odoriferous floures, but also that many by these violets receive ornament and comely grace; for there be made of them garlands for the head, nosegaies and poesies, which are delightfull to looke on and pleasant to smel ..."

Through their grace, beauty, and exquisite form, he adds: "[Violets] admonish and stirre up a man to that which is comely and honest ... for it would be an unseemly and filthy thing for him that doth looke upon and handle faire and beautiful things, to have his mind not faire, but filthy and deformed."[3]

I try to live up to that.

AS YOU WILL have gathered, in trying to achieve the perfect, yet carefree garden, I'm allowing—nay, encouraging—disorder. I am not a tidy gardener. Among my favourite practitioners of disorderly conduct are the weavers: plants that, in summer, meander randomly

The sweet violet holds its own in competition with other ground covers.

among the branches of spring-flowering shrubs or small trees, and redecorate them with fresh flowers.

In the first rank of performers of this trick are the *viticella* species of clematis. This climbing vine, native to Europe, was imported into English gardens in the reign of Queen Elizabeth I, the allegedly virgin queen, in whose honour it was commonly called "The Virgin's Bower." Later, the very famous, award-winning cultivar 'Etoile Violette' was developed. This is not the only *C. viticella* I grow, but it is the most vigorous, the most beautiful, the most reliable, hardy, disease- and trouble-free in its class. It's a star performer and plays a principal, serendipitous role in our garden—and should, I recommend, in yours, unless you prefer everything to be neat, tidy, and entirely under control. For in spring, 'Etoile Violette' will despatch scouts, three-metre-long twining shoots that wander through trees and shrubs within their reach, until they see the light, and terminate in a burst of five-centimetre flowers in imperial purple.

Randomly rambling clematis 'Etoile Violette'.

While blooming in sunshine, this scrambler likes a moist, shady root run. Ideal therefore to plant it at the base of the tree or shrub that you would like to redecorate when its own flowers are spent. I use 'Etoile Violette' to fill the branches of a pink dogwood (*Cornus florida*) and a Sargent crabapple (*Malus sargentii*), both small, spring-flowering trees. The clematis lies lightly on its host and does no harm. In winter, I cut it to its knees. The following spring it does it again, year after year.

Geranium 'Ann Folkard' is a weaver: a cranesbill, a sterile hybrid geranium with bright yellowish-green foliage and purple-magenta flowers. In summer it pushes out long shoots, rambling as it pleases over the ground in all directions. It delicately fills the surrounding space as it threads its way among adjacent herbaceous perennials, hiding bare patches and adding touches of colour to neighbouring plants. In winter, I cut back all of last summer's exploring shoots, leaving the evergreen central clump. In spring, the performance is repeated.

'Ann Folkard' is just one example of the many distinctive contributions that amateur gardeners, largely by chance, have made to the field of horticulture. Imagine the delight of the Reverend Oliver Folkard, an amateur gardener and a keen collector of hardy geraniums, when he discovered this infertile seedling in his Lincolnshire garden in 1973, the consequence of a happy accident, of unplanned hybridizing between two species. He named it for his daughter.

THERE ARE SEVERAL parts of our garden that I have surrendered entirely to serendipity. One, adjacent to our steep driveway, is an area that now most delightfully enacts the idea of letting Nature have her way. It started as a bank of fill: coarse sand and gravel, backed by a small forest of cedar and fir. I first used it as a parking lot for plants that I couldn't quite bring myself to throw out, but that needed to be moved from some other part of the garden. First installed was a daisy bush (*Senecio greyi*), an evergreen shrub endemic to New Zealand, a bully that had outgrown its space. Worse, it had the bad taste to produce yellow, daisy-like flowers, a poor combination with its grey leaves. (Had the flowers been white I'd have kept it, but eventually I threw

Dark-eyed 'Ann Folkard', a weaving geranium.

the whole thing out.) Other misfits, though originally plonked there because I had no other space that suited them, have, as they matured, serendipitously become woven into an appealing, leafy collage: a burning bush (*Euonymus alatus*), which turns a shockingly flagrant scarlet in fall; a self-sown arbutus; an evergreen honeysuckle (*Lonicera nitida*); Lewis's mock orange (*Philadelphus lewisii*), native to the Pacific Northwest; a black chokeberry (*Aronia melanocarpa*), native to Ontario and other parts east, which bears small white flowers in spring, shiny black fruit in summer—a feast for the birds—and colourful foliage in fall (in the case of the cultivar 'Autumn Magic'). An osmanthus, a spirea, and a red oak (*Quercus rubra*) have also found themselves parked there and the whole assembly in early fall puts on a display of foliage in tints of red, orange, brown, yellow, green: entirely unplanned, sheer serendipity.

Whatever soil there is came from the little I put in with the plants, supplemented with some fifteen years of decaying leaves and debris from nearby conifers. I never bother to clean this up. Beneath the shrubs lives a tangle of ground covers so thick that weeds have no chance. There's the English violet and its invasive companions, together with sprawling natives, such as pink-flowered, red-berried kinnikinnick (*Arctostaphylos uva-ursi*) and the dainty Pacific starflower (*Trientalis latifolia*). They all fight for space and light and I make no attempt to referee. May the best man win, as Nature takes her course. Along the edge, native bulbs—chocolate lilies, fawn lilies, and blue crown brodiaea—somehow manage to push their way through the thicket to bloom in spring. These have grown from seed I scattered there. Others, such as California poppies and lavenders, gave up the struggle upon encountering such remorseless competition.

At the foot of the driveway, where the sun shines, there's a mass of sea holly. With its metallic-blue, thistle-like flowers (a magnet for bees), and the surrounding, needle-sharp silvery bracts, it's an architectural beauty, up to a metre tall. The roots are deep and these self-seeding plants would become a weedy nuisance in more carefully cultivated parts of the garden; here, their spread is limited, because

Spectacular, carefree serendipity in spring. Who could ask for anything more lovely?

their seed is too heavy to be windblown, and I do not put the dead flowering stalks in the compost heap.

Occasionally, I wade in to snuff the fruit of bird droppings: a blackberry or salmonberry seedling. I may need to pull a snapweed (bitter cress) or wall lettuce that managed to survive and put out a flowering shoot. But these weedy intrusions are increasingly rare. Once a year I encourage fresh growth by cutting to the ground spent canes of the mock orange. Now and then I prune back shrubbery that hangs in the way of traffic. Other than that, the area receives nothing but neglect. It's never watered or fertilized. In all, I may spend at most three hours in a year tending this seventy-five square metres of undisciplined, disorderly border. It's all serendipity. Mother Nature has her way and—having set aside my own urge to take charge—I find her way surprisingly pleasing and, besides that, often pleasingly surprising.

Thus, I promote randomness, a specialty of Nature. Some may call it untidiness. I call it organized chaos.

Eryngium maritimum, sea holly.

Let the moss grow under your feet.

Hellebore and cyclamen, mingling in winter.

Serendipitous blending of epimedium and hellebore.

Organized chaos.

Salal, erythroniums, and anemone.

A chance seedling of *Hepatica nobilis*, liverleaf.

Plant an alpine dianthus in a crevice. Nature does the rest.

Serendipity through the camera lens: blue poppies and candelabra primulas.

I like rhododendrons informally interwoven with other shrubbery.

Sedums like moss too.

Different shrubs entwined: layers of accidental splendour.

I laid the foundations twenty years ago, when still young and strong!

14
A Plant in the Wrong Place

VISITORS OFTEN SAY, "YOU MUST spend an awful lot of time in this garden." (I generally interpret this as a veiled way of observing, "You must *waste* a lot of time in this garden.") "Sure," I reply, "It's my job. Don't you spend an awful lot of time on yours?"

The garden is twenty years old now and I am twenty years older and quite content to work in it, on average, about an hour a day. I made sure in the early years to do all the heavy lifting, especially the rockwork that defines the bones of this undertaking. I have no interest in further refining the array of trees and shrubs. I have no need to buy plants. I have not replaced my broken spade.

The goal of the strategy of embracing Nature as a partner, while choosing simplicity and encouraging serendipity, is to maintain the beauty of the place in all seasons and the pleasure it gives to Rosemary and me, while radically reducing the amount of time and work needed to keep it presentable. However, this does not include easygoing tolerance of weeds. You might argue they are part of Nature—but the very thought of this threw Mother into a purple hissy fit, so shrill I feared I'd blown even the small measure of understanding and cooperation I'd taken such pains to build.

"NO! NO! NO! Weeds are *not* part of Nature. They never have been. There are *no* weeds in the wild, or at least there weren't any before you and your kind, by one means or another, started moving plants from where they belong to where they don't. There are no *endemic* weeds. Even the idea of a weed is the outcome of your meddling. You won't find weeds in places distant from human habitation or undisturbed by human rapacity, like ranching or farming, logging or mining, not to mention your God-awful *gardening*. You won't find a weed *anywhere* in the wilderness. Must I remind you that you said as much yourself in describing your idea of the perfect garden? 'There's no call for weeding,' you said, 'because there are no weeds.'"

Right. She's always right. Over the years, I've hiked and walked in alpine meadows, deserts, woodlands, and forests; paddled a canoe in lakes and wild rivers; explored all manner of ecosystems on six continents and never looked at a plant thinking, "You don't belong here."

Mother Nature paused to collect her thoughts then, somewhat calmed, resumed her rant.

"When I say you will not find a weed in the wilderness, I'm particularly upset having to admit that even there, your weeds are putting down roots and acting like they belong. You call the process Naturalization, implying that I welcome these intruders, which I emphatically do not. I call it Occupation."

The University of British Columbia is on her side. It maintains an electronic atlas of the province that tracks those plants considered problem weeds, well over a hundred in all. "These are alien species . . . Some are highly invasive and alter natural ecosystems. Some of these plants are legislated as noxious under the BC Weed Control Act (either province-wide or regionally), or are designated by provincial agencies or invasive plant councils as nuisance, noxious, or invasive species and targeted for control."[1] On the list, these "alien species" are rated from bad to worse: from "abundant" (foxglove, herb robert), to "nuisance" (bindweed, St. John's wort), to "invasive" (butterfly bush, periwinkle), to "noxious" (gorse, orange hawkweed). The worst of all are both invasive and noxious: chief among them, Japanese knotweed.

Gardeners may be surprised to find a number of plants commonly grown in gardens on this list of weeds—the butterfly bush (*Buddleia*) for example. *I* was surprised to discover how many notorious *garden* weeds are not on the list, such as the common dandelion (*Taraxacum officinale*).

"Aha," said Mother. "That gets to the heart of our differences. You define a weed from a *gardener's* point of view. A weed to you is some pestiferous plant that invades your garden and you'd like to get rid of it—like the dandelion, which is actually rather pretty if you ever stop to take a close look at the intricate structure of the flower, not to mention the exquisite architectural symmetry of the blowball. Try to see it as I see it: I define a weed as any plant that invades *my* world, my wilderness, that undisturbed landscape that bears my name—Nature. So, even though they are an alien species, dandelions are not high on my hit list, nor on the UBC list, because they're not—as you put it—naturalized.

"To me a garden as a whole, dandelions included, is just a pile of pestiferous weed. Let me be perfectly clear: *as a whole* a garden is a noxious weed to my eye, and I won't put up with it, not on your nelly. I've cut you some slack, as I would for any gardener who tries to take me into account. Otherwise, just watch out—especially you lawn lovers."

Well, there's no refuting Mother Nature. All weeds are exotic. A weed is a plant in the wrong place. My imagined perfect garden, where no weeds grow, might possibly be realized in the Pacific Northwest, were it not for invasive exotics, at some time imported from distant lands, accidentally or on purpose. For none of our weeds evolved here.

There may be an exception to this rule: horsetail. Horsetail (*Equisetum*) is not on the UBC list. A Jurassic plant, horsetail has been on this planet so long that it's impossible to determine where in the world it originated. Australasia and Antarctica are ruled out: otherwise, horsetail must be regarded as a world citizen. It evolved somewhere in the supercontinent Pangea, millions of years before Earth's land mass took its present shape. It grew in the understorey of late Paleozoic forests and was probably browsed by dinosaurs.

Horsetail is a living fossil. I expect it will be with us until the crack of doom, several billion years from now, when the sun—in its pulsating death throes on the way to gravitational collapse as a neutron star—consumes its most favoured satellite, Earth, in a great ball of fire. Who knows: horsetail may even survive that. It has colonized every continent except Antarctica and, depending on the progress of global warming, may well be first in line for a passport to that part of the world. It is a plant of infinite resource and tenacity. It will hold its breath, dive under concrete pathways, and surface on the other side. Shoots of horsetail were the first plants to reappear on the slopes of Mount St. Helens following the 1980 eruption. It laughs off Roundup. It can regenerate itself from a fragment of elastic root and I have seen many new gardens and fresh commercial landscaping thus quickly and ineradicably infested. The usual source is imported topsoil. Another—sadly all too common—is bits of *Equisetum* root enclosed in the root ball of nursery-grown trees.

Procrastination saved our garden from horsetail. Once the house was finished, the surrounding space was built up with many truckloads of gravelly fill, topped with forty yards of soil, which was offered as "garden mix," made up of topsoil, probably scraped from other building sites, mixed with a lesser amount of rotted manure. It was described as "clean" and had indeed been sifted. I spread that mix the first summer, but left the garden unplanted. I had other things to keep me busy through fall and winter. Sure enough, come spring, it was easy to spot the feathery fronds of horsetail that surfaced here and there, sprouted from fragments of root that had fallen through the sieve. Before planting anything, I carefully extracted every piece, with associated root, and destroyed the weed in the fireplace. So there is no horsetail in our garden and no other heartbreaking perennial scourges, such as Japanese knotweed.

Horsetail, a worldwide weed.

"A WEED," SAID Ralph Waldo Emerson, "is a plant whose virtues have not yet been discovered."[2] Well, horsetail may make an excellent pot scrubber, but it is no less a plaguey weed for all that. On the other hand, Japanese knotweed was considered sufficiently virtuous to have been deliberately imported for ornamental cultivation. First, around 1840, it was introduced to Britain by the garden trade, which at the time was making handsome profits from the fashionable wealthy and their desire to show off the latest exotic plants from Asia. Victorian gardeners loved the two-metre-tall, leafy newcomer. After all, the bamboo-like stands, with fleecy flowering panicles, do have a certain elegance. And how were the plant collectors and nurseries that employed them to know that the plant they were importing and propogating was a thug? Fifty years later, it was introduced to North America.

Today, Japanese knotweed (*Fallopia japonica*),[3] is among the world's most notorious vegetative pests. The bloom has worn off, so to speak. Some years ago, a national poll voted it Canada's most noxious weed. We're not alone. Many countries have declared it an invasive species, to be shot on sight. It's incredibly difficult to get rid of. From an established clump, brittle roots run deep underground, sending up new shoots from nodes along their length. In this way a clump can infest an area several metres across and form satellite clumps that, in their turn, annex further territory. I have seen knotweed shoots pushing through blacktop. In preparing the ground for our (earlier described) garden of native plants, I took it on with mattock and spade and grubbed out the clumps with as much root as possible. It then took years of diligent pulling of every new shoot before the plant finally quit.

This menace has several common names: elephant ears, peashooters (a good use of the hollow stems), donkey rhubarb (a reference to the fact that someone would have to be as stupid as a donkey to try to eat it or think it was rhubarb, which it does vaguely resemble). It's called Japanese bamboo, American bamboo, Mexican bamboo, and BC bamboo.

Hancock's curse is a particularly apt name bestowed in Cornwall, England, where the plant spread from the property of a Mr. Hancock into a neighbouring garden, causing depreciation in the value of the invaded estate. Plants are often the cause of neighbourly squabbling—trees that block the sun or the view, overhanging branches, untidy hedges, invasive weeds—but that's another story. The moral here is "good fences make good neighbours," though in fact no fence would stop the dreaded knotweed.

So, not all weeds (a plant in the wrong place, remember) are uninvited. Some have been chosen: imported for botanical garden collections or brought in and propagated by the nursery trade for sale as ornamental plants. A most outstanding example of beauty turned beastly is the blue Nile lily (*Agapanthus sp.*), a native of South Africa, that has overrun bush land in the eastern states of Australia to the point of being declared a noxious weed. Thus, one country's cherished native plant may become another country's curse. Yet, Australians still plant it and in doing so, continue to provide it with an escape route into the wild.

Over time, I have ousted many determined perennial foes—knotweed, goutweed, bindweed, Himalayan blackberry, English ivy and feral holly, broom and gorse—but it seems I will never be rid of certain prolifically self-seeding annual or biennial garden weeds. While dense ground covers or layers of mulch have squelched their germination in much of the garden, I still have to deal with seeds blowing in the wind—primarily snapweed, wall lettuce, and grass.

Snapweed is also known as bittercress, for its edible leaves, or shotweed, for its hair-triggered habit of spitting fine seed into your eye as you stoop to pluck the plant. Hence another common name, touch-me-not. It's a small annual with a basal rosette and tiny white flowers. It can complete its pesky life, from sprouting to seed setting, in a matter of weeks. Unlike most annuals, which get one round in a year, snapweed gets two. The weeds of early spring will scatter seed that go forth and multiply in a fall crop.

They're easy to pull, but even then, if you leave them on the

Snapweed.

LEFT: Japanese knotweed.
RIGHT: Wall lettuce.

ground or put them on the compost pile, they often refuse to wither and die, and fight on, flowering, seeding, ensuring they will gain new territory when you spread your compost. Another source of snapweed is nursery-bought potted plants, wherein seeds often lie in wait on the surface.

There are just two good things to say about snapweed: first, it has a pretty botanical name, *Cardamine* (car-*dam*-in-ay), and second, the fresh leaves add a tasty, slightly spicy touch to a sandwich or salad. Otherwise, it has no virtue and I fight determinedly to get the upper hand. My approach is "see a weed, pull a weed." Occasional tours with bucket in hand keep the garden more or less snapweed-free year round.

Like this form of bittercress, most of our common weeds are uninvited and unwelcome aliens, without legitimate claim to residence in the Pacific Northwest, and certainly they have no place in the perfect garden. Once landed, though, some spread more successfully than in their homeland, because in the New World, the checks and balances that kept them under control in their original habitat are not in place.

Wall lettuce (*Lactuca muralis*) is another exotic import. I hate it. It's a native of Europe that has infested shady roadsides, woodland paths, and logged areas of the Pacific Northwest. Its seeds are blowing in the wind. If your neighbour has it, you have it. It's a relative of garden lettuce and it's edible, though the leaves are rather bitter and not to everybody's taste.

European grasses are weeds in our garden. Lawn-loving gardeners fret about ridding grass of moss, and may apply chemical and physical treatments to achieve this, sometimes to the point of obsession. My obsession is keeping grass out of moss. There's no chemical treatment. Pulling out the tufts before they go to seed is the means. I have spent hours on my knees to achieve this. I have been inspired by the temple gardens in Kyoto, Japan, where sheets of moss in piny woods are entirely free of grass and all other foreign objects; every scrap of litter, organic or inorganic, spent cherry blossoms, cigarette butts, even pine needles. Resident monks devotedly carry out this task. I would like to invite a score of them to spend a sunny afternoon in our garden.

By Mother Nature's standard, the biennial foxglove (*Digitalis purpurea*) is a weed, being among those alien plants that have become naturalized in the Pacific Northwest. *Pace*, Mother. I disagree. To quote Eeyore: "Weeds are flowers too, once you get to know them."[4] As a gardener, I do not perceive foxgloves as weeds, but rather as desirable flowers that need to be disciplined. On a warm day, they are a-buzz with bees that forage within the tubular flowers to gain the sweet nectar.

I don't plant foxgloves. Where they choose to grow is wherever the abundant seed falls, an instance of serendipity. Then I make the final choice, pulling up the seedlings in places I prefer not to see them. Best grown as a biennial, the tall spikes of purple, pink, or white flowers stand like marks of exclamation in the semi-wild garden. They may live on a year or two as short-lived perennials, but the flowers never again reach the towering splendour of the first blooming.

Yet beware the foxglove; its beguiling innocence conceals great peril. As Eeyore must have understood, all parts of the plant—leaves, flowers, stems, and roots—are poisonous, and potentially lethal if eaten. However, as is so often the case with Nature's poisons, the plants have therapeutic application, for foxgloves are the original source of the heart medicine, digoxin. The British botanist and physician William Withering made the discovery and published the first description of the use of digitalis derivatives in his 1785 book: *An Account of the Foxglove, and some of its Medical Uses; With Practical Remarks on Dropsy* [congestive heart failure], *and Other Diseases*.

All weeds are exotic. However, endemic plants may come to be regarded as weeds, or at least a nuisance, when the gardener chooses to grow them in unsuitably well-favoured soils or situations. There, they will seize the opportunity of spreading uncontrollably and smothering choice garden plants. For example, as I noted earlier, such natives as Pacific bleeding heart (*Dicentra formosa*) or redwood sorrel (*Oxalis oregana*) will run amok, scattering seeds and claiming

Redwood sorrel: a lovely native ground cover, best confined to poor soil in a wild area.

new territory with invasive roots madly running in all directions, just beneath the surface. That is to be expected. After all, weren't they here first? Even so, in such cases I have no hesitation in curbing Nature's inclination to take control. Yes, I do believe in letting Nature play her part, but, when push comes to shove, in the garden I'm still the boss.

15
Memory and Personality

I
T'S MORE THAN LANDSCAPE AND plants, though. The perfect garden, like the well-loved home, is rich in history, as well as memories of places visited, and of relatives and friends, living or dead.

In my grandparents' spacious garden in Cornwall, England, small, inscribed headstones, beneath a hedge of fragrant eucryphia, commemorated generations of dead dogs. In our Pacific Northwest garden, Phoebe and Carlo—both gluttons for affection most readily bestowed—rest in peace under a patch of dog-toothed violets (*Erythronium dens-canis*). Occasionally, I treat them to a sprinkling of bark mulch.

Ours is a garden of memories: a scrapbook of places visited, of people known and loved. Thus, the past shapes the present.

Memory, with its associated stories, is (along with simplicity and serendipity) at the heart of my idea of the perfect garden. To the physical dimension of the garden—space—memory adds a virtual dimension—time. This can be longer than the life of the garden, stretching back through the years by sparking warm memories of other gardens and other people long gone. More than once I have been shown a Christmas rose (a particularly long-lived plant) with an introduction such as, "That's a piece off a clump that my

A Christmas rose on Christmas Day—a somewhat battered, but much-loved Tigges family heirloom.

Scottish child, Sophie North.

grandmother had growing by her front door in the Old Country."
Thirty-five years ago, for example, Karin and Heinz Tigges dug a
hellebore, a Christmas rose, from his mother's garden in Westfalia,
Germany, and carried it off to Canada. Since then, it has moved with
them from home to home and is now retired in Roberts Creek, BC.

It follows that a garden can be a part of one's afterlife, insofar
as I believe that the only afterlife we get is held in the memory of
those who survive us. Similarly, in our garden, the English violets I
described earlier, imported from my long-dead maiden Aunt Betty's
garden in England, bring back affectionate images of her eccentric,
tweedy self and so are part of *her* afterlife.

In a garden, memory can take many forms. It may be attached to
favourite plants moved from a previously cherished garden, much as
family possessions go with the owner from home to home. It may be
held in a tree planted to mark the birth of a child. It may be embedded
in a piece of a precious plant from a friend's garden, for none are so
generous in sharing as gardeners.

In our garden there's a snowdrop that, to me, is particularly
meaningful, although in this instance I am two degrees of separation
from knowing the five-year-old child in whose memory the flower
was named 'Sophie North'.

In Dunblane, Scotland, on March 13, 1996, a man walked into
the primary school armed with four handguns. He made for the
gymnasium where he opened fire on a class of five- and six-year-olds.
Fifteen died, together with their teacher, who was trying to shield
them. Among the dead was Sophie North.

My remote connection with the child and this unimaginable crime
is through Evelyn Stevens, a friend who gardens near Dunblane and
knew the North family. Evelyn is a collector of snowdrops (*Galanthus*),
and some years earlier had noticed a unique, pure white variation
that had serendipitously arisen in her woodland. Having established
that this was indeed a new snowdrop, she registered *Galanthus
plicatus spp. byzantinus*, and later, following the massacre, renamed
it *G. plicatus* 'Sophie North'. Evelyn gave me a single bulb, which I

flew home to Canada and planted in our garden, since when it has gently multiplied. I treasure it.

I treasure other gifts from Evelyn that bring to mind memories of her and her garden in Scotland. She is a renowned and bemedalled plantswoman, especially admired as the holder of the national collection of that most coveted clan of flowering plants, the Himalayan blue poppy in all its variations. She has encouraged my obsession with these utterly alluring perennials (*Meconopsis spp.*), and has sent me fresh seed of the finest. On the two occasions that I've had the pleasure of spending time with her and her meconopsis collection, she has given me rooted divisions of *sterile* big blue perennial poppies— particularly handsome, named hybrids that have arisen randomly in gardens, mainly Scottish gardens, where the Asiatic poppies feel at home in a climate of post-nasal drip, damp and misty year round, with temperatures ranging from cool to cold. Not too different from life in the Himalayas. Being sterile, these hybrids spend no energy on reproduction and accordingly are more likely to be long lasting. They are unavailable in this country and, in accordance with Government of Canada regulations, must be imported with the roots washed clean of soil, treatment that would probably lead to a miserable end.

Therefore I have sneaked them in by means I prefer not to disclose, although I dare say the statute of limitations may apply. While the fertile blue poppies, whether species or hybrids, seem fated to be very short-lived in the Pacific Northwest—likely due to summer being too warm and too dry—the infertile hybrids do quite well here. I have three. In fact, blue poppies are the *only* plants I still grow that insist upon a degree of tender, loving care that is totally contrary to the principles laid out in this book. But I do love them so. The best of these, *Meconopsis* 'Mrs Jebb', bless her lovely heart, thrives and multiplies in our garden. We've been together now for eight years. I have shared her with other, younger blue poppy lovers, who may for years admire the perfectly formed azure flowers in their gardens each spring, and be reminded of—me.

Our garden is full of souvenirs of places we have been: of

Meconopsis 'Mrs Jebb'.

Sissinghurst Castle in Kent and its fabled garden created in the 1930s by Vita Sackville-West and her husband, Sir Harold Nicolson. Their son, Nigel Nicolson—then close to the end of his distinguished and controversial life—was walking in the garden when we visited in October 1999. Our paths crossed at the white garden and I asked if I might take a pod of ripe seed from the willow gentian (*Gentiana asclepiadea alba*), a rare variation with white, green-throated flowers. "Please do," he said. "Gardens should be shared." Back home, I grew the seed. Now, the white-flowering descendants of this little piece of Sissinghurst bloom in our garden each summer, alongside the common blue willow gentian.

Wherever we travel, I take a pocketful of small, plastic, pill containers. They're handy for seed collection, enlisting recruits that graduate in our garden as reminders. As a result, I see the Oyama magnolia (*Magnolia siebaldii*) well settled as a small flowering tree in our garden, grown from shiny red seed plucked from the botanical garden at Christchurch, New Zealand. It's the official flower of North Korea, a glimmer of joy in that otherwise dismal dystopia. I see *Cardiocrinum cordatum* var. *glehnii*, a Japanese relative of the giant Himalayan lily, gathered as seed from the botanical garden in Sapporo. And years ago, we rented a cottage for a week on the estate of Sleightholmedale Lodge, with its celebrated garden, an oasis huddled in a sheltered valley on the bleak Yorkshire moors. The owner, Rosanna James, showed us around and encouraged me to collect seed of the Oxford blue gentian sage (*Salvia patens*), the loveliest salvia of all. That was successfully raised in our garden, as its direct descendants have been ever since. For although *S. patens* is perennial (producing tubers, much like a dahlia), it's not frost hardy and is best started indoors in spring, from seed collected in fall. All it takes is a few seeds in a pot, on a windowsill. Okay, I admit it: I'm breaking my own no-bedding-plant rule. But for this salvia's heavenly blue, and the memories it summons of Sleightholmedale, I plead there's just cause to make an exception.

Even more important, Mrs. James invited me to take ripe seed pods of the species tulip, *T. sprengeri*, the red gem I raved about in Chapter Nine. That was the start of my interest in growing wild tulips.

Not all souvenirs survive. In Tasmania, I stuffed a tree-fern seedling into a pill container. At home it struggled for two or three years, managing a height of about fifteen centimetres before a particularly hard frost put it out of its misery.

In the garden, even the potato patch may hold memories. Pink Fir Apple is neither an apple nor a fir, but a knobbly, fingerling heirloom potato—a very old variety dating back to 1850. The tubers are pink, the flesh butter yellow and waxy with a distinctive nutty flavour. Once you grow this potato, you never want to be without it. In our garden and our kitchen, it's a remembrance of a holiday in the Scilly Isles, where we celebrated Rosemary's fiftieth birthday. The proprietor of our B&B served them with dinner and gave us one to take home. It proved to be prolific and we harvested our own the following summer. At the local Saturday farmers' market, I showed one to a grower who had previously worked for the Canadian Food Inspection Agency as an enforcer of Acts and Regulations. He roundly scolded me for illegally importing the thing, thus putting the entire Canadian potato industry at risk, all the way from British Columbia to Prince Edward Island—then asked if he could have some. Now he sells Pink Fir Apples by the bushel.

OVER TIME, A house becomes a home through the accumulation of memory. Can a house without a garden become a home? Not for me. But Ms. Bountiful couldn't give a fig about memory. "As far as I'm concerned that's all sentimental tosh." Nor could she care less about my sentiment that the perfect garden has character, reflecting the gardener's personality and interests. "Totally irrelevant."

On visits to England, I loved strolling along the street where my sister lived in the southern suburbs of London. The houses were semi-detached, perhaps six metres wide, and each had a pocket front garden, separated from the sidewalk by a low brick wall. There were rose gardens and water gardens with little fountains; gardens with a flowering cherry or plum as a centrepiece; peony gardens; gardens of bedding plants—daffodils and tulips alternating with petunias and salvias. There were gardens with trellises for clematis, climbing roses, and honeysuckle; gardens of fragrance and gardens of plastic gnomes and pink flamingos. Each was unique, lovingly kept, and each in its own way was the proud and personal expression of the householder's joy of gardening. They were, I imagined, also gardens of memory.

It was a delight to walk down the street, stopping to admire each little Eden. I put this in the past tense, because, alas, starting in the 1980s, one by one, these small front gardens have been paved or bricked over to provide parking: two cars per family. The collective loss of street personality in suburban London—not to mention the loss of bird and butterfly habitat and the flooding resulting from so much hardscape—is an environmental disaster, yet hardly recognized because the change crept over the street very gradually, over a period of thirty years.

In cities such as Vancouver, in neighbourhoods rich and poor, a slow but noticeable change is under way: the gradual increase in the number of front gardens along residential streets, replacing erstwhile patches of grass, typically bisected by a concrete path and steps leading to the front door. Wealthier neighbourhoods have taken the lead, but in these areas street-front gardens are likely to be laid out and maintained by a landscape designer, with the obligatory greensward mown to a perfect length, walls and rocks artistically placed, clipped hedges, weeping maples, and ornamental conifers arranged exactly so—a bit like a house that's been "staged" for selling. Attractive, yes, but there's a sense of conformity, and accordingly a muting of personality.

More interesting to me are the less wealthy neighbourhoods, where the lots are narrow and the practice of cultivating the land between the house and the sidewalk is gaining popularity. The results may rank no better than private soldiers in the hierarchy of garden design, but they do usually say something about the personality, creativity, likes and dislikes, as well as the interest—or lack of interest—of the resident gardener. Sometimes, they will give a hint of the owners' ethnic background and culture. So we find tiny front gardens decorated with a merry throng of spring bulbs, or planted with evergreen ground covers, or devoted to flowers of a particular colour (yellow is a favourite), or shaded with a wooden lattice, interlaced with vines. The variety is endless. Prepare for surprises as you explore the streets of East Vancouver. Where there's sun, I've seen small front gardens laid out in rows of carefully tended vegetables. Occasionally, these individual miniature landscapes may be without plants, such as a hardscape of pebbles of different size, with found sculptures of twisted driftwood and slabs of granite.

Quite often, the homeowner has enlarged the canvas by requisitioning the boulevard, the strip of city-owned property between the sidewalk and the pavement. So far, the city turns a blind eye to this guerrilla gardening, despite probable bylaw infractions. It's all in keeping with enlightened contemporary ideas of urban farming: green roofs, backyard chickens, beekeeping, sustainability, permaculture, and the proliferation of local farmers' markets.

Such gardens proclaim the *passion* of its maker for gardening and for plants. For this alone, the efforts of all those committed to gardening deserve admiration and respect—even if the choice and arrangement of plants and colours, may, in the eye of the beholder, add up to a discordant clamour. For when it comes to the ardent gardener, proudly showing off her accomplishments, whether or not it appeals to me really doesn't matter.

To her it's perfect, or at least headed in that direction.

16
Letting Nature Play Her Part

I'VE BEEN A GARDENER FOR more than half a century. Looking back, I see that I've spent decades happily, but aimlessly, lurching from one obsession to the next. In my first garden, I assigned a great deal of space to orderly ranks of dahlias galore: the bigger, the more elaborate, the better—cartwheel-sized dahlias in all colours. They would march forth in late summer like a parade of gaudy clowns. They all had to be dug up every fall, the tubers cleaned and divided, packed in peat moss and stored over the winter in a cool but frost-free place. In spring, I would turn over the soil before replanting the tubers, adding fertilizer and spreading slug bait to be sure those sneaky slimeballs didn't chew at the new shoots. So much work. Of course, for most of the year there was nothing to see. I must have been out of my mind. I forgive myself only because I was young. As Joshua Reynolds said, "Taste does not come by chance: it is a long and laborious task to acquire it."[1]

In my thirties, I spent many a winter evening browsing catalogues in search of fancy cultivars of tall bearded irises, aiming to collect as many different colours as possible, then assigned parts of the garden—whole beds if necessary—exclusively for their cultivation. I remember, back in the 1960s, buying all the different cultivars of Oriental poppy I could find, giving me a brief flourish of Oriental splendour in June and bare earth for the rest of the year. A specialist nursery on Vancouver Island fed that particular craze. It was all about flowers and all about colour. To me, stem and leaves had but one purpose—to hold the flowers up. I have double-dug beds for hybrid tea roses which, in winter, displayed nothing but wreckage. I have filled the summer garden with nursery-bought bedding plants: petunias, pelargoniums, and impatiens. I have been through the rhododendron craze, the fancy tulip craze, and the "mum" craze. I was a floweraholic, a kid in a candy store—couldn't drive past a nursery without dropping in. As for botanical Latin, that was for garden snobs. I had no appreciation whatsoever of its poetic precision and eloquence in describing a plant's provenance, history, or principal characteristic in just two words.

Over the years, various influences gradually amended this passion for floral kitsch. I started to grow up in my late forties, when my mother gave me a membership to the Royal Horticultural Society (RHS). With this came a fine monthly magazine and, most important, a seed exchange, with overseas members entitled to thirty packets at no cost. The catalogue arrived each fall, listing seed of some fifteen hundred trees, shrubs, perennials, bulbs, and annuals—all collected from RHS gardens and packaged by volunteers. The problem was that each entry was listed on just one line in its botanical (scientific) name, without illustration or description. It was all Greek to me. Line by line, I had to refer to a botanical encyclopaedia to learn what all this was about and to be sure I was not inadvertently selecting crabgrass. I learned.

In particular, I learned to grow all I need from seed, whether started outside in pots or in the basement under lights. I experimented with unfamiliar plants. Typically, in a given year, one third would succeed and two thirds fail. In this way, over time, I built a reliable repertoire of less common bedding plants, as well as perennials seldom available in neighbourhood garden stores. So, though no less a mad keen gardener, I have become, I regret to say, a very poor customer for nurseries, purchasing little other than bales of sterile, peat-based compost for starting seed and, on occasion, fertilizer.

Growing my own saves money. It is above all richly satisfying. It has also pretty well put a stop to the accidental importing of seeds of unwanted weeds, eggs of unwelcome pests, and spores of unwanted diseases. From even the most scrupulous suppliers, such stowaways may find their way to the garden.

THROUGH MOST OF my life as a gardener I have assumed, as a matter of course, that I was in charge. Gardeners do like to feel they're in control. They seek to impose order. Therefore the idea of letting Nature play a part is counterintuitive, because it requires embracing a measure of *dis*order (although that is not how Mother Nature sees it).

Furthermore, while I have proposed some tactics for enacting this strategy—welcoming native plants, choosing simplicity, exploiting serendipity—there are no rules that define it. It's how you *think* about a garden. Rather than a product, letting Nature play her part is a process: a strategy recognized, adopted, and applied in gardening to one extent or another, while still reflecting the particular genius and tastes of the gardener.

Aging, too, has compelled me to reconsider my approach to gardening: to see that letting go does not mean giving up. So I have, as I said, thrown out the spade, given away the mattock. I never stake a perennial; if the wind blows it over, let it lie. I don't buy bedding plants and I don't buy bulbs—just let the ones I have multiply as Mother Nature wills. I don't fret about deer: the very few that visit are welcome to nibble the kale. There's not much else they seem to covet—after all, they're used to sharing habitat with native plants. I don't clean up fallen leaves, except on pathways, and the leaves I do collect are scattered among the shrubbery to help suppress weeds. I don't mow, because there's no lawn to mow. I really don't mind if the salal or the sweet woodruff gets a little out of hand. I let the moss grow under my feet. It is indeed both a carefree and a care-*free* garden, yet still a very much cared-*for* garden.

I feel that in recent years, I have found a focus that quite pleases me year round. There was no *eureka* moment, but rather a slow understanding and pulling together of various influences. Plant hunting in Tibet was very important: recognizing in those mountain meadows what I labelled the perfect garden, yet not a garden, but a work of Nature; realizing (to repeat what I wrote at the start) that these sublime wilderness settings "can provide us with the inspiration—in imitation of Nature—to work toward the state of ecological equilibrium that the perfect garden represents."

Other gardeners and their creativity have opened my eyes to ideas of balance and structure, and to the beauty of form and texture in foliage, branch, and bark. Our own good fortune in possessing a little bit of the West Coast that is, of itself, so richly endowed with rock, different elevations, moss and lichen, native shrubs and trees, that it simply *insists* upon close collaboration with Nature—that has been very important too.

Tying these influences together is the acceptance that Nature must be invited to play an equal role in the garden and that it is wise, up to a point, to let things go *her* way. Really, it's an awful lot less work.

Let *her* do *her* share of the work, I say. The result may not be the perfect garden; like the end of the rainbow, that never can be reached. I wouldn't know what to do if I did—reach it. Who could imagine a gardener wiping his hands, hanging up the secateurs, removing his boots, surveying the scene, and saying, "Well that's that. I've made it, the perfect garden. There's nothing left to do."

APPENDIX

Here is a selection of plants that should flourish with little or no attention in the Pacific Northwest and that well suit the model of the carefree, perfect garden—especially for their simplicity (all but two are species) and their inclination to reproduce by seed, often with unplanned results (serendipity). This list is not comprehensive. I have chosen these plants because I have grown *all* of them from seed with little difficulty, and they have proved to be long lasting and trouble free in the garden. Besides, I like them.

In Chapter Seven, I described my way of growing *native* bulbs from seeds. That technique works well for other bulbous plants listed here, such as tulips, narcissus, fritillaries, and lilies. It will also work for non-bulbous herbaceous perennials. However, for large seeds, such as peony, cyclamen, and hellebores, I suggest placing just a few on the compost surface before adding the grit. Otherwise, when it comes time to transplant, you may confront a thicket of roots, impossible to disentangle without damage.

As for fine seeds, such as primula or ramonda, I fill the pot to the top with sterile compost, then scatter the seed thinly and gently press or rub it into the surface. No grit is required.

My way is Nature's way, more or less. Other techniques for starting seed include stratification: using the fridge for a month or two, to speed up the process by fooling the seed into believing it has endured winter and accordingly will break dormancy earlier. As much as a year may be saved in the wait for germination. In some cases, indoor grow lights or a cool greenhouse may speed the process. Experiment by all means.

(* denotes a plant native to the Pacific Northwest)

Allium
AA. *acuminatum** (tapertip onion), *cernuum** (nodding onion), *flavum*.

Anemone (windflower)
AA. *blanda* (Grecian windflower), *hupehensis* (Japanese anemone), *nemorosa* (European wood anemone).

Aquilegia (columbine)
A. *formosa** (crimson columbine).

Brodiaea
BB. *coronaria** (crown brodiaea), *hyacinthina** (fool's onion).

Camassia (camas, wild hyacinth)
CC. *leichtlinii,** *leichtlinii alba,** *quamash** (camas).

Cornus (dogwood)
C. *canadensis** (bunchberry, creeping dogwood).

Cyclamen (cyclamen)
There are twenty-three species in all. Those that naturalize most freely are C. *coum* (late winter flowering) and C. *hederifolium* (late summer, early fall). Others that are hardy but less prolific are CC. *cilicium, graecum, libanoticum, mirabile, purpurascens*.

Dianthus (pink)
DD. *alpinus* (alpine pink), *pavonius* (peacock-eye pink).

Dierama (wandflower)
D. *pulcherrimum* (angel's fishing rod).

Dictamnus (gas plant, false dittany, Fraxinella)
D. *alba*.

Dodecatheon (shootingstar)
DD. *pulchellum** (pretty shootingstar), *hendersonii** (broad-leaved shootingstar).

Eranthis
  E. hyemalis (winter aconite).

Erythronium
  *EE. oregonum** (white fawn lily), *revolutum** (pink fawn lily).

Eryngium (eryngo, sea holly)
  E. maritimum (sea holly).

Fritillaria (fritillary)
  FF. acmopetala (pointed petal fritillary), *affinis** (chocolate lily), *camschatcensis** (black lily, northern rice root), *graeca, meleagris* (snake's head fritillary), *pallidiflora*.

Fuchsia
  F. procumbens (creeping fuchsia).

Gentiana (gentian)
  GG. asclepiadia (willow gentian), *asclepiadia* var. *alba*.

Hacquetia
  H. epipactis.

Helleborus (hellebore)
  HH. argutifolius (Corsican hellebore), *foetidus* (stinking hellebore, bear's foot), *x hybridus* (Lenten rose), *lividus, niger* (Christmas rose).

Hepatica (liverleaf)
  H. nobilis.

Hyacinthoides (bluebells)
  H. hispanica (Spanish bluebell).

Libertia (libertia)
  LL. grandiflora, peregrinans.

Lilium (lily)
  *LL. columbianum** (Columbian lily), *formosanum* (Taiwanese lily), *henryi* (tiger lily), *martagon* (Turk's cap lily), *pardalinium* (leopard lily), *parryi* (lemon lily), *pumilum* (coral lily).

Candelabra primulas from seed.

Lobelia (lobelia)
LL. *cardinalis* (cardinal flower), *syphilitica* (great blue lobelia), *tupa* (devil's tobacco).

Narcissus (narcissus, daffodil, jonquil)
NN. *bulbocodium* (hoop petticoat daffodil), *cyclamineus* (cyclamen-flowered daffodil), *jonquillia* (rush daffodil).

Oxalis (wood sorrel)
O. *oregana** (redwood sorrel).

Paeonia (peony)
Herbaceous perennials: PP. *anomala, cambedessedesii* (Majorcan peony), *emodi* (Himalayan peony), *japonica* (Japanese peony), *mairei, mascula* (Balkan peony), *obovata* (woodland peony), *mlokosewitschii* (golden peony, Caucasian peony), *veitchii* (Veitch's peony). Woody species (tree peonies): PP. *delavayi, lutea, rockii.*

Paradisea (paradise lily)
PP. *liliastrum* (St. Bruno's lily), *lusitanica.*

Primula

Candelabra primulas: *PP. beesiana* (candelabra primrose), *bulleyana*, *florindae* (Tibetan cowslip), *japonica* (Japanese cowslip), *prolifera* (glory-of-the-marsh), *pulverulenta* (mealy cowslip), *wilsonii*. Other primulas: *PP. sieboldii* (Japanese primrose), *veris* (cowslip), *vulgaris* (primrose), *x juliae* 'Wanda'.

Ramonda

R. myconi (Pyrenean violet).

Scilla (squill)

SS. bifolia var. *rosea*, *siberica* (Siberian squill, wood squill).

Thalictrum (meadow rue)

T. delavayi (Yunnan meadow rue).

Trillium (wake-robin)

TT. ovatum* (western trillium), *rivale* (snow trillium).

Tulipa (tulip)

TT. batalinii, sprengeri (Sprenger's tulip), *sylvestris* (wild tulip), *turkestanica* (Turkestan tulip).

Viola (violet)

V. odorata (sweet violet).

Many of these seeds will be hard to come by. Few will be found on garden centre seed racks, fewer still in supermarkets. Some may be obtained from mail-order catalogues. Another source is botanic gardens, some of which package and sell seed collected on site. Best of all are seed exchanges run by horticultural societies, wherein members from around the world contribute seed they have collected from their gardens and in the wild. Packages are then distributed free, though only to members. So join up and pay your dues!

Two such societies in the Pacific Northwest are: the Alpine Garden Club of BC, www.agc-bc.ca, and the Northwest Perennial Alliance, www.northwestperennialalliance.org.

Magnolia x brooklynensis, 'Woodsman'.

NOTES

Opening Quotation
1. Thomas Jefferson. Letter to Charles Willson Peale. August 20, 1811.

Chapter 2: The Perfect Garden
1. *The Works of Sir Joshua Reynolds*, 4th edition (1809). Discourse on Art 1, number 3, delivered on December 14, 1770.
2. Michael Pollan. *Second Nature: A Gardener's Education*. Grove Press, New York, 2007, p. 37.

Chapter 4: Let the Moss Grow Under Your Feet
1. Alexander Pope. *Epistles to Several Persons: Epistle IV to Richard Boyle, Earl of Burlington*, 1731.
2. Michael Pollan. Op. cit., p. 37.

Chapter 6: The Floristic Kingdoms
1. Antarctic hair grass (*Deschampsia antarctica*) and Antarctic pearlwort (*Colobanthus quitensis*). There are, besides, around a hundred species of moss, twenty-five liverworts, and three to four hundred lichens.

Chapter 7: Rewilding
1. Quoted in Stephen E. Ambrose. *Undaunted Courage: Meriwether Lewis, Thomas Jefferson and the Opening of the American West*. Simon & Schuster, New York, 1996, p. 369. (Though Lewis was a fine soldier and a brave explorer, it appears, from reading his journal, that he was a poor speller.)

Chapter 8: The Double-flowered Salmonberry
1. Hummingbirds are uniquely adapted to high-speed drinking. Tube-like channels, running the length of the forked tongue, trap the nectar by curling around it. The liquid is then drawn into the throat, as the tongue flicks in and out at a rate up to twenty times per second, enabling the bird to drink several times its body weight in the course of a day!

Chapter 9: The Lilies of the Field
1. David Fairchild. *The World Was My Garden: Travels of a Plant Explorer*. Charles Scribner's Sons, New York, 1938.
2. *The Bible*. Matthew 6:28-29. Gerard's source would have been a translation preceding the King James version (1611). Many modern translations prefer "flowers of the field," or simply "wildflowers"—no doubt including tulips.
3. *Gerard's Herbal*. Marcus Woodward, editor. Bracken Books, London, 1985, p. 33.

Chapter 11: The Twelfth Wedding Anniversary Flower
1. E.H.M. Cox. *Plant Hunting in China*. Collins, London, 1945, p.116.

Chapter 12: It Isn't Easy Being Green
1. Gisela Schmiemann. *Helen Ballard—The Hellebore Queen*. Edition Art and Nature, Cologne, 1997.
2. "It's Not Easy Being Green." Lyrics by Joe Raposo. 1970.
3. Quoted in *Northern Traditions*, Gwendolyn Toynton, editor. Numen Books, Australia, 2011, p. 80.

4. *Gerard's Herbal.* Op. cit., p. 233.
5. John Cook. Letter published in *The Town and Country Magazine, or Universal Repository of Knowledge, Instruction and Entertainment.* February 1769, London, p. 135.
6. Sir Robert A. Christison. *A Dispensatory, or Commentary on the Pharmacopoeias of Great Britain: comprising the Natural History, Description, Chemistry, Pharmacy, Actions, Uses, and Doses of the Articles of the Materia Medica.* Lea & Blanchard, Philadelphia, 1848.

Chapter 13: Serendipity
1. *Gerard's Herbal.* Op. cit., p. 196.
2. *Invasive species in Garry oak and associated ecosystems in British Columbia.* www.goert.ca
3. *Gerard's Herbal.* Op. cit., p. 198.

Chapter 14: A Plant in the Wrong Place
1. www.geog.ubc.ca/biodiversity/eflora/
2. Ralph Waldo Emerson. *Fortune of the Republic. Lecture delivered at the Old South Church. March 30, 1878.* The Riverside Press, Cambridge, Massachusetts, 1879, p. 8.
3. This genus is named for Gabriele Fallopio, or Fallopius (1523-1562), superintendent of the botanical garden at Padua. In yet another instance of the confluence between botany and medicine, Fallopius was also one of the most important anatomists of the sixteenth century. He was the first to describe the fallopian tube. The tube-like structure of Japanese knotweed no doubt prompted the choice of *Fallopia* as a scientific name.
4. A.A. Milne. *Winnie the Pooh.* Methuen & Co. Ltd, London, 1926.

Chapter 16: Letting Nature Play Her Part
1. John Northcote. *The Life of Sir Joshua Reynolds.* Henry Colburn, London, 1819, p. 264.

ACKNOWLEDGMENTS

In the front matter of this book, there's a page that few take time to scan. It's a page of formal copyright claims and legal disclaimers, dates, numbers, registration details, and assurances that the paper is acid free and the ink vegetable based. You may safely lick these pages.

In the midst of all this small print are credits, recognizing, among others, TouchWood Editions' editor, Marlyn Horsdal. That name should be in bold type, to emphasize the indispensable part that Marlyn played in the final stages of writing this book and the other three that we've worked on together over the last few years. I especially appreciate her wise counsel and think of her as a partner in the enterprise.

TouchWood's designer, Pete Kohut, also deserves his name set in bold. I'm grateful to him for the devoted care and creativity he has brought to the final assembly of this book, the third we have worked on together. His marriage of text and illustration in an eye-catching layout ensures a tantalizing first impression as prospective buyers flip through these pages.

In all, the TouchWood team, now energetically and enthusiastically led by Taryn Boyd, has once again provided me with support, encouragement, and professional advice. Working with this publishing house is always stimulating.

I thank all those whose ideas and experience I continue to learn from: creative artists in the garden, who have over the years shared their passion, their knowledge, their experience, and their plants with me. Ever optimistic, ever generous, gardeners are, as Des Kennedy said, "a special breed."

And finally, a tip of the hat to Mother Nature.

BILL TERRY is a retired CBC executive, as well the author of *Blue Heaven: Encounters with the Blue Poppy* and *Beyond Beauty: Hunting the Wild Blue Poppy* and co-author of *Beauty by Design: Inspired Gardening in the Pacific Northwest*. He lives on British Columbia's Sunshine Coast with his wife, Rosemary Bates. To find out more, visit www.meconopsis.ca.

A great blue heron stands sentry on our shoreline.